100 Quick Quizzes

Camilla de la Bedoyere

Miles Kelly

First published in 2010 as *Flip Quiz: General Knowledge Ages 7–8* by Miles Kelly Publishing Ltd
Harding's Barn, Bardfield End Green, Thaxted, Essex, CM6 3PX, UK

Copyright © Miles Kelly Publishing Ltd 2010

This edition published in 2013

2 4 6 8 10 9 7 5 3 1

Publishing Director Belinda Gallagher
Creative Director Jo Cowan
Assistant Editor Claire Philip
Cover Designer Jo Cowan
Designers Jo Cowan, Joe Jones
Junior Designer Kayleigh Allen
Image Manager Liberty Newton
Production Manager Elizabeth Collins
Reprographics Stephan Davis, Jennifer Hunt, Thom Allaway

ISBN 978-1-78209-123-3

Printed in China

A[...] [...]ary

The publis[...] [...]otographs:

Dreamstime.com Quiz 9 ([...] [...]skaya, (8) Alexandre Fagundes
De Fagundes, (9) Kojoku[...] [...]yfarer; 97 Julia Taranova;
Quizzes 51–60 section bars ar[...] [...]tz, (9) Darren Hester; 28 giona;
32 Liveshot; 35 3desc; 36 [...] [...].54, (9) Roman Ivaschenko,
(10) A. Marcynuk; 40 (6) khz, (8) **Askews & Holts** [...]r Nolan; 59 (4); 60 (2) Joe Gough,
(5) Paul Cowan, (6) Foodlover[...] [...]tares, (4) Kwest, (5) Fatman73,
(8) Konstantin Yuganov, (9) Ph[...] [...]4; 89 (7) dave timms, (8) Tommy
Schultz, (9) Sulabaja, (10) Brian [...] [...]vshill; Quizzes 41–50 section bars
Martha **Getty Images** Qu[...] [...]) Mikhail Kondrashov, (5) Troy
Kennedy; 32 Matthew Cole[...] [...]:harov Dmitry; 89 (6) jerome
whittingham; 90 (6) suemac[...] [...]der; 100 (8) Majoros Laszlo,
(9) Drazen Vukelic; Quizzes 71[...] [...]:ric **Administration (NOAA)**
Quiz 7 David Burdick

All other photographs are from: digitalSTOCK, digitalvision, John Foxx, PhotoAlto, PhotoDisc, PhotoEssentials, PhotoPro, Stockbyte

All artwork from the Miles Kelly Artwork Bank

Every effort has been made to acknowledge the source and copyright holder of each picture.
Miles Kelly Publishing apologises for any unintentional errors or omissions.

Made with paper from a sustainable forest

www.mileskelly.net info@mileskelly.net

www.factsforprojects.com

100
Quick
Quizzes

CONTENTS

How to play
Read these pages before you start

Living World • Quizzes 1–10
All about animals and plants

Healthy Living • Quizzes 11–20
About your body and keeping fit and well

Wonderful Words • Quizzes 21–30
This section will test your knowledge of English

Super Science • Quizzes 31–40
A great section for budding scientists

Number Crunchers • Quizzes 41–50
Good at maths? Then you'll love this section

Our World • Quizzes 51–60
All about the wonderful world we live in

Past Times • Quizzes 61–70
This will test your knowledge of history

How We Live • Quizzes 71–80
A fun section about people around the world

True or False • Quizzes 81–90
A quick-fire section about lots of different topics

Lucky Dip • Quizzes 91–100
A mixed bag with lots of different subjects – great fun!

Scorecards
Ten scorecards to record your results

HOW TO PLAY

To start

Choose which section you want to play. There are 10 sections, 10 quizzes per section and 10 questions per quiz.

Player/team 1 will always play odd-numbered quizzes – 1, 3, 5, 7 and 9.
Player/team 2 will always play even-numbered quizzes – 2, 4, 6, 8 and 10.

Question & Answer quizzes

Quiz number
There are ten quizzes
in each section.

Questions
There are ten
questions per quiz.

Illustrated fact
Learn a new fact to
amaze your friends.

Flash symbol
This symbol means that the
opposite quiz has a Picture
clue to help you to answer.

Section heading
There are ten
subject sections.

Answers
Cover up the answers
before you start.

Picture clue
This image will help you
answer a question on
the opposite quiz.

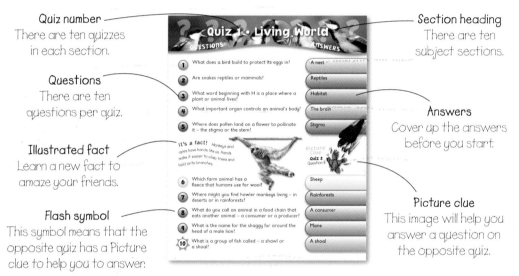

Playing on your own

Cover up the answers before you start. You will play all eight Question & Answer quizzes and fill in your scorecard.

Playing with a friend or in teams

See how Claire and Simon play to help you with your game.

1. Simon covers up Quiz 2 so Claire can't see it while she asks him questions on Quiz 1.
2. Claire asks Simon Questions 1–10 of Quiz 1.

3. For each correct answer, Claire adds a tick to his scorecard. For each incorrect answer, Claire leaves the space blank.
4. Simon asks Claire Questions 1–10 of Quiz 2.
5. Simon fills in Claire's scorecard.
6. Once they have answered all ten questions each, they add up the final score to see who wins that game.

Picture Challenge quizzes

Playing on your own

Cover up the answers before you start. You will play both Picture Challenge quizzes and fill in your scorecard.

Playing with a friend

Claire and Simon reach the last two quizzes in the section, 9 and 10.

1. They cover up the answers before they start.
2. Claire shows Simon the pictures for Quiz 9.
2. Simon writes down his answers on a piece of paper.
3. Claire checks Simon's answers to see how many he has got right and gives him a tick for each correct answer.
4. Then it's Simon's turn to challenge Claire. She will complete Quiz 10.

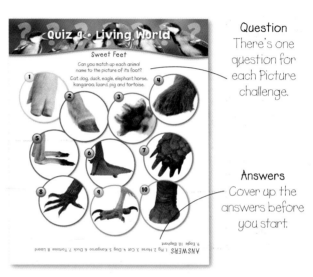

Question
There's one question for each Picture challenge.

Answers
Cover up the answers before you start.

Scorecards

Photocopy the scorecards instead of writing in the book, so you can play again and again. Don't forget — for each section, you'll need one scorecard for each player.

Fill in the quiz numbers.

Add a tick for each correct answer.

Write the player or team name.

Quiz Number	1	2	3	4	5	6	7	8	9	10	Quiz Score
1	✔	✔		✔			✔				4
3	✔		✔	✔	✔			✔	✔		6
5		✔		✔		✔	✔	✔		✔	6
7	✔		✔	✔	✔	✔		✔	✔	✔	8
9		✔			✔		✔	✔			4

Player: Claire   **Total: 28/50**

Count up the ticks in each row and fill in the score.

Add up the quiz scores to work out your final score.

Quiz 1 • Living World

1 What does a bird build to protect its eggs in?

A nest

2 Are snakes reptiles or mammals?

Reptiles

3 What word beginning with H is a place where a plant or animal lives?

Habitat

4 What important organ controls an animal's body?

The brain

5 Where does pollen land on a flower to pollinate it – the stigma or the stem?

Stigma

It's a fact! Monkeys and apes have hands, like us. Hands make it easier to climb trees and hold onto branches.

Picture Clue
Quiz 2
Question 6

6 Which farm animal has a fleece that humans use for wool?

Sheep

7 Where might you find howler monkeys living – in deserts or in rainforests?

Rainforests

8 What do you call an animal in a food chain that eats another animal – a consumer or a producer?

A consumer

9 What is the name for the shaggy fur around the head of a male lion?

Mane

10 What is a group of fish called – a shawl or a shoal?

A shoal

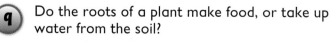

Quiz 2 • Living World

 1 Do mushrooms make food from sunlight, or do they feed on dead things?

They feed on dead things

 2 What word beginning with P describes a stage in a caterpillar's development into a butterfly?

Pupa

 3 What word beginning with G describes the point at which a seed begins to grow?

Germination

 4 Which of these living things will be at the top of this food chain: rabbit, fox or grass?

Fox

 5 Which bird is bigger, an eagle or a wren?

An eagle

It's a fact! Many types of plants die down and rest during winter. Trees that lose their leaves in autumn are called deciduous.

Picture Clue
Quiz 1
Question 10

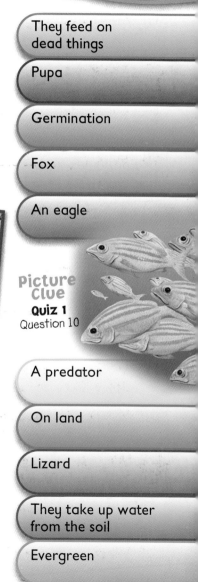

 6 Is an animal that hunts other animals called a predator or a terminator?

A predator

7 Did dinosaurs lay eggs on land or in water?

On land

8 Is a gecko a type of lizard or a type of beetle?

Lizard

9 Do the roots of a plant make food, or take up water from the soil?

They take up water from the soil

 10 What word beginning with E is given to plants that keep their leaves all year?

Evergreen

Quiz 3 • Living World

 1 What word beginning with A is the group of animals that includes frogs, toads and newts?

Amphibians

 2 Why do frogs have webbed feet?

To help them swim

 3 In plants, what do ovaries grow into, fruits or leaves?

Fruits

 4 What is a male sheep called?

A ram

 5 Do plants need oxygen or helium to survive?

Oxygen

It's a fact! Plants have been growing on Earth for at least 400 million years. Scientists know about early plants by studying fossils, the remains of plants that have turned to stone.

Picture Clue
Quiz 4
Question 1

 6 Where do acorns come from, oak trees or elm trees?

Oak trees

 7 What type of teeth do animals use to cut and slice their food – molars or incisors?

Incisors

 8 What word beginning with C are animals that we get meat, milk and leather from?

Cattle, or cows

 9 What is the biggest animal on the planet?

The blue whale

10 How many legs does a spider have?

Eight

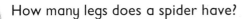

Quiz 4 • Living World

 1 Which large, tree-living mammal has reddish fur, very long arms and grasping hands and feet?

Orang-utan

 2 What word beginning with S is a protective leaf that grows around a flower bud?

Sepal

 3 What animal do we get pork from?

Pig

 4 Where do most frogs lay their eggs, in water or on land?

In water

5 Do seeds need warmth to start growing?

Yes

It's a fact! Spiders belong to a group of animals called arachnids. Most catch their prey using fang-like mouthparts, and kill them by injecting poison.

Picture Clue
Quiz 3
Question 4

 6 Where might you find a woodlouse living, under a rock or in the sea?

Under a rock

 7 Is an iris a type of flower or a type of frog?

A type of flower

 8 What word beginning with V is the poison that some snakes and spiders use to kill other animals?

Venom

9 When do most plants grow best, in summer or in winter?

Summer

 10 Birds keep their eggs warm to help their chicks grow. Is this called germination or incubation?

Incubation

Quiz 5 • Living World

 1 Which of these animals does not lay eggs: sparrow, crocodile, ostrich or kangaroo?

Kangaroo

 2 Does cotton come from a plant or from an animal?

It comes from the cotton plant

 3 What is the female part of a flower called, a carpet or a carpel?

A carpel

 4 Kelp is a type of plant that grows in the oceans. Is it also called seaweed or seaflower?

Seaweed

 5 What word beginning with B are tiny living things that can cause disease and make food go off?

Bacteria

It's a fact! Seaweeds are used to make many things, from toothpaste to ice cream to make-up.

Picture Clue
Quiz 6
Question 1

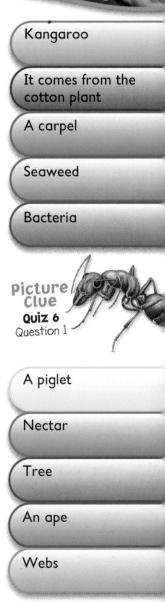

 6 What is a baby pig called?

A piglet

 7 What word beginning with N is a sweet liquid that flowers make to attract insects?

Nectar

 8 Sycamore, willow and birch are all types of what?

Tree

 9 What type of animal is a gorilla?

An ape

 10 What do spiders build with silk to help them catch their prey?

Webs

Quiz 6 • Living World

 1 What type of animal has six legs and a body that is divided into three parts?

An insect

 2 Where do potatoes grow, underground or hanging from a tree?

Underground

 3 What is the name for the male part of a plant that is covered in pollen – the anther or the antler?

The anther

 4 Is a leopard a spotted cat or a stripy cat?

Spotted

 5 What are a lion's long, pointed teeth called?

Canines, or fangs

It's a fact! Scientists have already found and studied one million different types of insect, and they discover about 10,000 new types every year!

Picture Clue
Quiz 5
Question 2

 6 Which bird lays the biggest eggs?

Ostrich

7 What are animals that eat meat called, carnivores or carnivals?

Carnivores

 8 Do plants wilt when they are growing towards the Sun, or when they are dying?

When they are dying

 9 What word beginning with Y is a type of fungus that is used to make bread?

Yeast

 10 Would you be more likely to find a cactus living in a dry habitat or a wet one?

A dry habitat

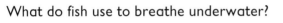

Quiz 7 • Living World

QUESTIONS **ANSWERS**

 1 What word beginning with E describes an animal or plant that might soon become extinct?

Endangered

 2 Do plants need sunlight to make food and grow?

Yes

 3 What do fish use to breathe underwater?

Gills

4 Do cockerels lay eggs?

No, because they are male. Hens lay eggs.

 5 What name is given to baby swans – signals or cygnets (say: sig-nets)?

Cygnets

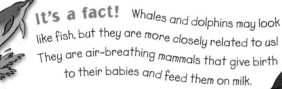 **It's a fact!** Whales and dolphins may look like fish, but they are more closely related to us! They are air-breathing mammals that give birth to their babies and feed them on milk.

Picture Clue
Quiz 8
Question 9

 6 Are sharks fish or whales?

Fish

7 Why do most flowers have petals – to protect growing seeds or to attract insects?

To attract insects

 8 Snowy, barn and tawny are all types of what?

Owl

 9 Which habitat best suits a crab – a forest or a seashore?

A seashore

 10 What word beginning with P describes when pollen reaches the female part of a flower?

Pollination

Quiz 8 • Living World

 1 Cod, haddock, salmon and herring are all types of what?

Fish

 2 Which are the parts of a plant that grow underground?

Roots

 3 Are elephant herds led by females or males?

Females

 4 Where is food made in a plant – in its leaves, flowers or roots?

Its leaves

 5 What word beginning with S is a time of deep rest for most animals?

Sleep

It's a fact! Animals often use colours, patterns and unusual body shapes to help them hide in their surroundings. This is called camouflage.

Picture Clue
Quiz 7
Question 8

 6 Bacteria and viruses are tiny living things, but which is smaller?

Viruses

7 Which one of these birds can fly: kiwi, emu, hawk or ostrich?

Hawk

 8 What colour is good camouflage for animals living in the Arctic?

White, to blend in with the snow

9 Are sea cucumbers animals or plants?

Animals

10 Where do bees live, in hooves or hives?

Hives

Quiz 9 • Living World

Sweet Feet

Can you match up each animal
name to the picture of its foot?

Cat, dog, duck, eagle, elephant, horse,
kangaroo, lizard, pig and tortoise.

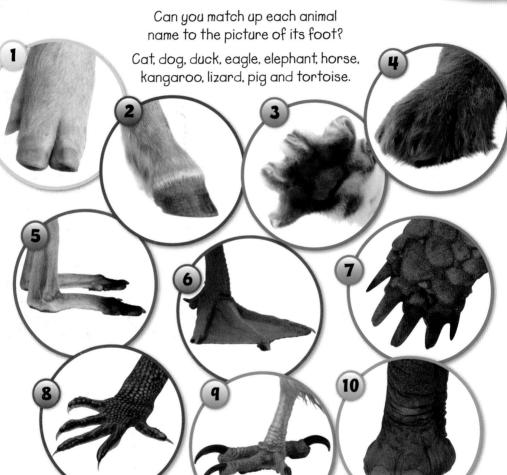

Animal Cousins

Animals that are closely related often look
very similar. Can you tell these cousins apart?

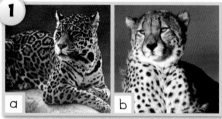

1 a · b

cheetah and leopard

2 a · b

chimp and gorilla

3 a · b

fox and wolf

4 a · b

tortoise and turtle

5 a · b

goose and swan

Quiz 11 • Healthy Living

 1 What is the name of the stretchy organ in which food is broken down into smaller bits?

Stomach

 2 Which of these is not a disease: measles, hay fever, chicken pox or mumps?

Hay fever

 3 Where is the largest muscle in your body?

In your bottom

 4 If you exercise, will your heart wear out faster, or get stronger?

Get stronger

5 What kind of breath do people have if they don't brush their teeth?

Bad breath

It's a fact! Ears are much more complicated than they look. The visible part on the side of your head is called a pinna and it helps to direct sound into the ear canal.

Picture Clue
Quiz 12
Question 6

 6 What word beginning with H is a big plastic hoop that you can swivel around your hips?

Hula

 7 Is spinach a green leafy vegetable or a spice?

A green leafy vegetable

 8 Does a healthy diet contain some fat, or no fat at all?

Some fat

 9 How many teeth do children have – 20 or 40?

20

 10 Why do people have earwax?

To protect their ears and keep them clean

Quiz 12 • Healthy Living

QUESTIONS

ANSWERS

1 What word beginning with B is the red liquid that runs through arteries and veins?

Blood

2 Which of these foods is the best source of protein: meat, tomatoes or rice?

Meat

3 If you have a cold, what should you use every time you sneeze?

A tissue

4 What chemical is used in toothpaste to stop teeth from decaying, fluoride or flavour?

Fluoride

5 Is it good for parents to smoke in the same room as their baby?

No, they shouldn't smoke at all

It's a fact! Calcium is an essential mineral for our bodies. It is necessary for many life processes, including growth, and it is also used to build strong teeth and bones.

Picture Clue
Quiz 11
Question 7

6 What racket game is played with a shuttlecock?

Badminton

7 How many livers does a person have?

One

8 Recipes usually have a list of all the items needed to cook a dish. What are these items called?

Ingredients

9 What does a pedometer measure, your heartbeat or your footsteps?

Footsteps

10 What word beginning with C is an important mineral that people get from drinking milk?

Calcium

Quiz 13 • Healthy Living

1 What are our large grinding teeth called?

Molars

2 Why should you wash your hands after using the toilet?

To remove any bacteria (germs)

3 Which vitamin helps your bones to grow, vitamin C or vitamin D?

Vitamin D

4 What word beginning with K is the organ that cleans the blood and makes urine?

Kidney

5 When you exercise, does your heart pump blood around your body more quickly or more slowly?

More quickly

It's a fact! Kidneys take unwanted chemicals and water out of your blood and send them to your bladder. When your bladder is full it stretches, and your brain tells you to visit the toilet.

Picture Clue
Quiz 14
Question 10

6 Which of these foods has the most fat: lentils, broccoli or butter?

Butter

7 What is the name of the bony case that protects the brain?

The skull

8 I am a white vegetable with brown skin and I can make you cry. What am I?

An onion

9 What colour is an avocado?

Green

10 Is alcohol a drug or a vitamin?

A drug

Quiz 14 • Healthy Living

QUESTIONS

ANSWERS

 1 What is the name for the part of your leg between your knee and your hip?

Thigh

 2 Why should medicines be kept out of the reach of children?

Because they can be poisonous

 3 What word is used to describe a woman who has a baby growing inside her?

Pregnant

 4 How many teeth do most adults have?

32

 5 Roughly how many calories can you burn by walking for one hour – 230 or 160?

230

It's a fact! A newborn baby is helpless and cannot do anything for itself. By the time a baby is nine months old, it can usually crawl and perhaps even stand.

Picture Clue
Quiz 13 Question 7

 6 What gas do humans need to survive?

Oxygen

 7 What word beginning with R appears on the skin if it is irritated, causing it to be sore or spotty?

Rash

 8 Which vitamin, found in dairy foods and carrots, helps you to see in dim light?

Vitamin A

 9 Why is it best to keep meat in the fridge or freezer?

To stop bacteria making it go bad

10 I am a type of food containing protein and vitamins. I have a shell and a yolk – what am I?

An egg

Quiz 15 • Healthy Living

1 What word beginning with I is a tooth that is used for cutting and slicing food?

Incisor

2 Is the area around your hips called a pelvis or an elvis?

A pelvis

3 When you breathe in, to which organs does the air travel to?

To your lungs

4 As we get older does our skin become wrinkly or smoother?

Wrinkly

5 Does your brain need to sleep?

Yes, it does

It's a fact! Most people get hiccups, but no one knows why for sure. The best way to get rid of them is to change your breathing rhythm, which is why it helps to breathe very slowly and deeply.

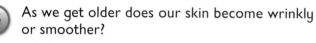

Hic!
Hic!

Picture Clue
Quiz 16
Question 9

6 What would you eat to get Vitamin C – oranges or fish fingers?

Oranges

7 Does exercise make you breathe faster or slower?

Faster

8 What name is given to a point where two bones meet and move?

Joint

9 Does smoking cause heart disease?

Yes

10 Where would you find a person's nostrils?

In their nose

Quiz 16 • Healthy Living

QUESTIONS

ANSWERS

 1 What muscle beginning with C lies at the back of your leg, between your knee and your ankle?

Calf

 2 Do teeth have roots or shoots?

Roots

 3 What word beginning with K is a tough material that makes up your hair and fingernails?

Keratin

 4 Which of these is not a water sport: tobogganing, kayaking or snorkelling?

Tobogganing

5 Where would you find your taste buds?

On your tongue

It's a fact! Tobogganing, skiing, skating, snowboarding and ice hockey are all winter sports that require snow or ice. They feature in the Winter Olympics, which take place every four years.

Picture Clue

Quiz 15
Question 3

 6 Do breakfast cereals contain vitamins and minerals?

Yes

 7 Which exercise is best for building bigger muscles – walking or swimming?

Swimming

 8 What word beginning with M is a type of gentle cream you can use to treat dry skin?

Moisturiser

 9 What is the name of the protective gear sportspeople wear to protect their heads?

Helmets

10 How many months are women pregnant for?

Nine

Quiz 17 • Healthy Living

1 What word beginning with S is a ball-and-socket joint that lets your arm move in all directions?

Shoulder

2 Why do people sweat?

To cool down

3 What name is given to the soft, pink flesh that surrounds your teeth?

Gums

4 What organ pumps blood around the body?

Heart

5 Which type of bread has the most fibre in it – white or brown?

Brown

It's a fact! Human bodies need to be at just the right temperature. If you get too hot or too cold you can become ill. The best temperature is 37°C.

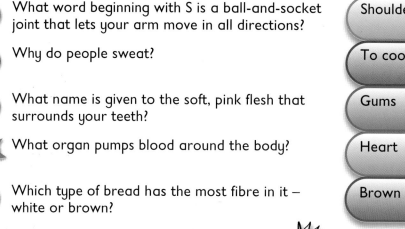

Picture Clue
Quiz 18
Question 10

6 What equipment would you need if you were rowing a boat – oars or sails?

Oars

7 Which sport is best for building strength – dancing or weightlifting?

Weightlifting

8 Where in the body is the iris, pupil and lens?

In the eyes

9 Which sport is best for keeping you flexible – gymnastics or motor-racing?

Gymnastics

10 What is the largest organ of the human body?

Skin

Quiz 18 • Healthy Living

QUESTIONS

ANSWERS

1 What is the joint in your arm, between your shoulder and your wrist?

Elbow

2 What name is given to the time when children develop into adults – pupating or puberty?

Puberty

3 What is the best way to get vitamins – by taking pills or by eating a balanced diet?

By eating a balanced diet

4 What is the name of the gas that we breathe out?

Carbon dioxide

5 Who needs the most sleep, children or adults?

Children

It's a fact! Burps, or belches, happen when you have swallowed too much air or have had a fizzy drink. It is your body's way of getting rid of that air before it travels further into your body.

Picture Clue
Quiz 17
Question 4

6 Which sharp, pointed tooth is called a fang in some animals?

Canine

7 What is the name of the chemical in cigarettes that people get addicted to, carotene or nicotine?

Nicotine

8 Which of these is not a martial art: karate, tae-kwondo, hoi-sin or judo?

Hoi-sin (it's a sauce!)

9 What would you eat to get Vitamin B – green vegetables or sweets?

Green vegetables

10 What type of cream should you use to protect your skin in the sunshine?

Sunscreen or sun cream

Quiz 19 • Healthy Living

Name that Fruit

Fruit is great because it not only tastes delicious, it's good for you too!

Can you name each of these fruits?

ANSWERS 1. Peach 2. Pear 3. Cherries 4. Strawberry 5. Lemon 6. Kiwi 7. Grapes 8. Apple 9. Bananas 10. Pineapple

Quiz 20 • Healthy Living

Name that Sport

Taking part in a sport can be a great
way to have fun and stay healthy.

Can you name each of these sports?

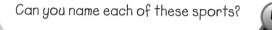

Quiz 21 • Wonderful Words

1 Is the letter 'v' a vowel or a consonant?

A consonant

2 Would you scratch an itch or itch a scratch?

Scratch an itch

3 What word beginning with C is a punctuation mark you would use between items in a list?

Comma

4 What type of animal is Curious George?

A monkey

5 If something is velvety, is it smooth or rough to touch?

Smooth

It's a fact! One of the oldest words in the English language is 'apple'. Other ancient words include 'tin', 'bad' and 'gold'.

Picture Clue
QUIZ 22
Question 1

6 What vegetable carried Cinderella to the ball?

A pumpkin

7 Spell 'dragon'.

Dragon

8 What word beginning with F describes a large area of trees?

Forest

9 Is the word 'old' an adjective or a noun?

An adjective

10 Where do suffixes go, at the end of a word or at the beginning?

At the end of a word

Quiz 22 • Wonderful Words

QUESTIONS

ANSWERS

1 What type of factory did Willie Wonka own?

A chocolate factory

2 If the weather is described as gusty, is it snowing or windy?

Windy

3 Would you use a telescope or a microscope to see something far away?

A telescope

4 Spell 'adventure'.

Adventure

5 What did Little Bo Beep lose?

Her sheep

It's a fact! Monday is named after the Moon, and Sunday is named after the Sun. Wednesday is named after a Saxon god called Woden.

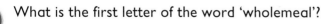

Picture Clue
Quiz 21
Question 6

6 What name is given to a block of sentences – parachute or paragraph?

Paragraph

7 Lucy Cousins wrote the Maisy stories. What type of animal is Maisy?

A mouse

8 What is the first letter of the word 'wholemeal'?

W

9 If you were living in the 'lap of luxury' would you be comfortable or miserable?

Comfortable

10 Would you take a boat or a car into a harbour?

A boat

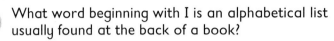

QUESTIONS

ANSWERS

 1 Spell 'pretend'.

Pretend

 2 What word beginning with I is an alphabetical list usually found at the back of a book?

Index

 3 Is 'dancing' a verb or a noun?

A verb

 4 Who wrote stories about Noddy and Big Ears?

Enid Blyton

 5 How many 'e's are in the word 'referee'?

Four

It's a fact! Written by Michael Bond, the first Paddington Bear book was published in 1958. Paddington books have sold more than 35 million copies.

Picture Clue
Quiz 24
Question 1

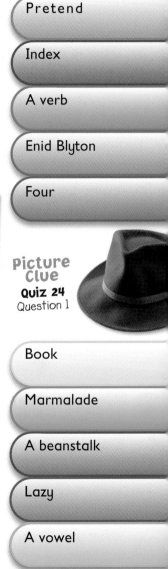

 6 Hardback, paperback, fiction and non-fiction are all types of what?

Book

 7 What type of sandwiches does Paddington Bear love?

Marmalade

 8 What plant did Jack climb to reach the giant's castle?

A beanstalk

9 If a person is lackadaisical (say: lack-a-day-si-cal) are they energetic or lazy?

Lazy

10 Is the letter 'e' a vowel or a consonant?

A vowel

Quiz 24 • Wonderful Words

QUESTIONS

ANSWERS

 1 Which cat did Dr Seuss write about?

The Cat in the Hat

 2 What word describes a book you can listen to – rodeo or audio?

Audio

 3 What word beginnng with A is the place where you live?

Address

 4 If you lived for one century, how old would you be?

One hundred

 5 Would you use a skidoo to travel on snow, or to hit a ball?

To travel on snow

 It's a fact! The Horrible History books are amongst the most-borrowed books in British libraries. They are popular all over the world and are translated into 20 languages!

Picture Clue
Quiz 23
Question 8

 6 What type of history does Terry Deary write about, Horrible or Hairy?

Horrible

 7 What name is given to conversations in a book – diagram or dialogue?

Dialogue

 8 If your skin is tender, is it painful or dry?

Painful

 9 Spell 'cupboard'.

Cupboard

10 What word beginning with I is a person who does the drawings for a book?

Illustrator

Quiz 25 • Wonderful Words

1 Which of these words doesn't end in the letter 'b': thumb, dumb, hum, crumb?

Hum

2 What word beginning with C is a person in a story?

Character

3 Who wrote the book *Matilda*?

Roald Dahl

4 What word beginning with P is a funny play performed at Christmas?

Pantomime

5 What is a fiasco – a total failure or a type of dancing?

A total failure

It's a fact! The Victorians based their pantomimes on fairy tales. It is traditional for the main male character, such as Aladdin or Prince Charming, to be played by a woman.

Picture Clue
Quiz 26
Question 5

6 Spell 'amazing'.

Amazing

7 What word beginning with A is punctuation that is used to show that a letter is missing?

Apostrophe

8 Which mythical magician took care of King Arthur?

Merlin

9 How many index fingers do you have?

Two

10 If a person 'goes berserk', are they angry or happy?

Angry

Quiz 26 • Wonderful Words

QUESTIONS

ANSWERS

1 What type of stories is Aesop famous for?

Fables

2 Where do prefixes go – at the end of a word or at the beginning?

At the beginning

3 Is 'laptop' a noun or a verb?

A noun

4 If the day is sweltering, would you feel hot or cold?

Hot

5 What is the name of Peter Pan's worst enemy?

Captain Hook

It's a fact! Aesop was a slave who lived in ancient Greece more than 2000 years ago. His fables (stories with messages), such as the 'Tortoise and the Hare', are still popular today.

Picture Clue
Quiz 25
Question 8

6 Who writes the *Captain Underpants* stories?

Dav Pilkey

7 What word beginning with J is a person who rides horses for a living?

Jockey

8 Spell 'school'.

School

9 Is an encyclopedia a book of facts or maps?

A book of facts

10 Who wrote about Peter Rabbit and Jemima Puddleduck?

Beatrix Potter

QUESTIONS

ANSWERS

 1 Which mythical creatures are half women, half fish?

Mermaids

 2 What word is 'flu' short for, influenza or influx?

Influenza

 3 What type of witch does Jill Murphy write about?

The Worst Witch

 4 What is the name of the wooden puppet that dreamt of becoming a real boy?

Pinocchio

5 What is Horrid Henry's perfect brother called?

Perfect Peter

It's a fact! Legends of mermaids and mermen have been told since the days of the ancient Greeks. They also appear in old Egyptian and Irish stories.

Picture Clue
Quiz 28
Question 3

 6 Would you drive a juggernaut, or cook with it?

Drive it, it is a huge lorry

 7 Spell 'silence'.

Silence

 8 What name is given to a page of a book – a loaf or leaf?

Leaf

 9 What types of punctuation are known as '66' and '99'?

Quotation or speech marks

10 If someone is described as all 'skin and bones' do they look fat or thin?

Thin

Quiz 28 • Wonderful Words

1 Which bear is Piglet's best friend?

Winnie the Pooh

2 How many letter 't's are in the word 'mattress'?

Two

3 Which famous dancing mouse is taught by Miss Lilly?

Angelina Ballerina

4 If someone is 'bewildered' are they invisible, or confused?

Confused

5 What is the opposite of freezing?

Boiling

It's a fact! The tales of Winnie the Pooh and his friends were written by A A Milne. His son, Christopher Robin, had a tubby teddy bear, which was just like Pooh.

Picture Clue
QUIZ 27
Question 4

6 Which punctuation mark would you use to show surprise?

An exclamation mark

7 What is the beginning of a report called, the introduction or the conclusion?

The introduction

8 Which of these words starts with the letter 'k': knee, nowhere, nappy?

Knee

9 Is the letter 'w' a consonant or a vowel?

A consonant

10 Is a miniature horse very tall or very small?

Very small

A Piece of Cake!

Idioms are little phrases we use in our speech, all the time. Use the clues to complete these common idioms:

1 An 🍎 a day keeps the doctor away.

2 🐜 in your pants.

3 It makes my 👋 curl.

4 Turn over a new 🍃.

5 💀 in the closet.

6 The green-eyed 🐉.

7 When the cat's away, the 🐭 will play.

8 Made of 🪙.

9 It's the 🐝 knees.

10 Don't let the 🐱 out of the bag.

Quiz 30 • Wonderful Words

Tell the Tale

Use the picture clues to help you identify ten fairy tales and stories:

Quiz 31 • Super Science

 1 What is the opposite of hard?

Soft

 2 People make me by weaving threads together and use me to make clothes. What am I?

Fabric

 3 Does a skateboard use electricity?

No

 4 If there's light in front of you, where is your shadow – underneath you or behind you?

Behind you

5 What is paper made from?

Trees

It's a fact! When it is heated to high temperatures, glass becomes soft. This makes it possible to mould it into different-shaped things such as bottles.

Picture Clue
Quiz 32
Question 8

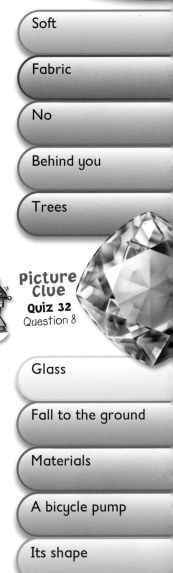

6 What word beginning with G is a material you can see through, and is made by heating sand?

Glass

 7 Does gravity make things float, or fall to the ground?

Fall to the ground

 8 Glass, metal, wood and paper are types of what?

Materials

 9 If your bicycle tyres were flat, what tool would you use to fill them up with air again?

A bicycle pump

 10 When you twist, stretch or bend something what are you changing – its colour or its shape?

Its shape

Quiz 32 • Super Science

QUESTIONS

ANSWERS

 1 Are aluminium drinks cans magnetic?

No

 2 Which reflect light better – shiny things or dull things?

Shiny things

 3 Which material would make the worst knife – plastic, paper or metal?

Paper

 4 Are some magnets stronger than others?

Yes

 5 What word beginning with P is the opposite of push?

Pull

It's a fact! Some magnets, like those used in scrapyards, are so strong they can pick up a car. These are special 'electro' magnets that are switched on and off using electricity.

Picture Clue

Quiz 31
Question 2

 6 Which is heavier, one kilogram of feathers or 500 grams of stones?

One kilogram of feathers

 7 Does a paperclip have magnetic poles?

No, only magnets have poles

 8 I am a sparkling precious stone that is very hard. People put me in jewellery. What am I?

A diamond

9 What is the name of the simple spring used to fire arrows?

A bow

10 Can loud sounds damage your hearing?

Yes

Quiz 33 • Super Science

 1 Is human hair flexible?

Yes

 2 If you skate along a flat road, what word beginning with F will eventually make you stop?

Friction

 3 Which of these things is not magnetic: a pin, a pencil or a key?

A pencil

 4 Which feels colder to touch with your fingers — metal or wool?

Metal

 5 If something is transparent, what is it?

See-through

It's a fact! When jumping, a flea can accelerate more than 20 times faster than a launching space shuttle. Its muscles contain a material called resilin, which makes its back legs act like catapults.

Picture Clue
Quiz 34
Question 5

 6 When our side of the Earth is facing the Sun, do we have daytime or night time?

Daytime

 7 Why do some saucepans have plastic handles?

So they don't get too hot to touch

 8 I am made of metal, but you can squash me and I bounce back to my original shape. What am I?

A spring

9 Why aren't mops made from metal foil — because metal is too shiny or because it isn't absorbent?

Because it isn't absorbent

 10 Do you use a pushing or a pulling force to bowl a cricket ball?

A push

Quiz 34 • Super Science

1 When does the Sun make longer shadows – at midday or in the evening?

In the evening

2 Which of your senses do you use to tell if something is quiet?

Hearing

3 If something allows electricity to pass through it, is it a conductor or a condor?

A conductor

4 Why wouldn't a lead balloon float in air?

Because lead is very heavy

5 Which is closest to the Earth – the Moon or the Sun?

The Moon

It's a fact! You can use the Sun's shadows and a sundial – the oldest scientific instrument – to tell the time. The Sun is always in the same place at a particular time of day, so shadows always fall in the same direction.

Picture Clue

Quiz 33
Question 8

6 Will a magnet help you stick a piece of paper to a wall, or to a fridge?

To a fridge

7 What kind of lines does light travel in – straight or curved?

Straight

8 If you really stretch a spring, is there a strong or weak force pulling it back?

Strong

9 Why does a rubber welly boot sink when a rubber beach ball floats?

Because air in the ball is lighter than water

10 Which rock can be used to write on a blackboard: slate, chalk or marble?

Chalk

Quiz 35 · Super Science

 1 What word beginning with P are the ends of a magnet?

Poles

 2 Which is most likely to conduct electricity – a stone, a paperclip or a piece of cotton wool?

A paperclip

 3 What is the name for water that falls from the sky?

Rain

 4 If you rub a balloon it will stick to a wall. Is this because the rubbing makes glue or electricity?

Electricity

 5 Does friction make something move faster or slower?

Slower

It's a fact! Materials that electricity can't pass through are called electrical insulators. Mains electricity is dangerous, so wires are covered with insulating plastic, to keep electricity safely inside.

Picture Clue
Quiz 36
Question 2

 6 What word beginning with S is a dark area made by a solid object blocking out light?

Shadow

 7 Why do sports people usually drink from plastic rather than glass water bottles?

Plastic is lighter and less likely to break

 8 If you push a pram harder, will it move faster, slower or at the same speed?

Faster

9 What word beginning with R describes magnets that are pushing each other apart?

Repelling, or repulsion

 10 I am a soft, stretchy material that grows on sheep. What am I?

Wool

Quiz 36 • Super Science

 1 Why can't you make a spring out of glass?

Glass is not flexible and would break

 2 What can't be made from plastic: a comb, a magnet or a pair of sunglasses?

A magnet

 3 Which man-made material can be hard or soft, transparent or opaque, and has many uses?

Plastic

4 Where is a magnet strongest – at the poles or in the middle?

At the poles

5 Is stretching a rubber band a reversible change?

Yes

It's a fact! In the late 19th century, billiard balls were made from ivory (elephant's tusks). John Wesley Hyatt invented a plastic that could be used instead, saving thousands of elephant's lives.

Picture Clue
Quiz 35
Question 10

6 What is the opposite of magnetic?

Non-magnetic

 7 Will a heavy person sink into a trampoline more than a light person, or less?

More

 8 Why is aluminium metal great for making rockets and planes?

It is strong and light

 9 Is petrol made from oil or from rock?

Oil

10 What do you use to turn lights on or off – a switch or a stitch?

A switch

Quiz 37 • Super Science

QUESTIONS

ANSWERS

1 Is a metal coin easier to squash than a sponge?

No, a sponge is much easier to squash

2 Is magnetism a force or a movement?

A force

3 I am hard and shiny and don't break easily. What material am I?

Metal

4 Which will bounce best – a warm tennis ball or a cold one?

A warm one

5 Which lets through the most light, plain glass or coloured glass?

Plain glass

It's a fact! A blacksmith works with the metals iron and steel. The metal is heated, then tools are used to hammer, bend and cut it. Blacksmiths make things such as horseshoes.

Picture clue
Quiz 38
Question 10

6 Will a magnet's south pole attract the south pole of another magnet?

No, it will repel it

7 Why is metal useful for making ships' anchors?

Because it is heavy

8 I am a clear liquid that all living things need to survive. What am I?

Water

9 What tool would you use to force a nail into a piece of wood?

A hammer

10 If you break a magnet in half, will one half have the north pole and the other half the south pole?

Each part will have a north and south pole

QUESTIONS

ANSWERS

1 If you compress something are you squashing it or blowing it up?

Squashing it

2 Which of these fabrics are made from chemicals in a factory: wool, nylon, polyester and cotton?

Nylon and polyester

3 When water comes out of a tap what state is in – liquid, solid or gas?

Liquid

4 Does paper need air or light before it can burn?

Air

5 What is the best material for making chairs – wool or wood?

Wood

It's a fact! Mirrors look like they give out light, but they actually bounce it back to you. A mirror is just a thin, smooth layer of metal on the back of a sheet of glass.

Picture Clue
Quiz 37
Question 7

6 Is gravity a force?

Yes

7 Which tool would you use to turn a screw so it goes into a piece of wood?

A screwdriver

8 Hot water comes out of the hot tap. Where is it heated, in the kettle or in the boiler?

In the boiler

9 Is temperature measured in metres, degrees Celsius or kilograms?

Degrees Celsius

10 When a liquid becomes a solid, has it frozen or melted?

Frozen

Make or Reflect?

Some things make light, but other things reflect light. Look at each of these objects and say whether they make light or reflect light.

ANSWERS 1. Make 2. Reflect 3. Make 4. Reflect 5. Make 6. Make 7. Reflect 8. Reflect 9. Make 10. Make

Quiz 40 • Super Science

How See-through am I?

How well does light pass through these objects? Say for each one whether they let LOTS of light through, SOME light through, or if they BLOCK light out.

1 What number comes next in this sequence: 20, 40, 60 ...?

80

 2 If one spider weighs half a gram, how much do 10 spiders weigh?

5 grams

 3 Lee gets £5 pocket money a month. How much money does he get in six months?

£30

 4 I have 8 corners, and 6 faces that are all the same size. What 3D shape am I?

A cube

5 Add 8 + 12 + 4 + 6.

30

It's a fact! It takes the Earth 365¼ days (one year) to travel once around the Sun. Every four years we add the quarter days together and get one extra day.

Picture Clue
Quiz 42
Question 7

 6 Max was born in 1999. How many candles did he have on his birthday cake in 2008?

9

 7 What is 5 x 5?

25

 8 How many right angles are in a right-angled triangle?

1

 9 What is 15 less than 100?

85

 10 If a clock chimes every quarter of an hour, how many times will it chime in one hour?

4

Quiz 42 · number Crunchers

1 What is double 55?

110

2 Katy buys 2 books for £4 each and gets £2 change. How much money did she start with?

£10

3 What is half of 60?

30

4 Add 20 + 30 + 40 + 10.

100

5 A bus leaves Newby Town bus depot every 5 minutes. How many leave in one hour?

12

It's a fact! Before money was used, people swapped goods, such as cows and food. This swapping was called bartering. Shells, nuggets of silver and shovels have all been used as money in the past!

Picture Clue

Quiz 41
Question 4

6 What is 10 x 3?

30

7 How many lines of symmetry does a rectangle have?

2

8 What is longer, one metre or 50 centimetres?

One metre

9 Thirty-two children are going on a trip. If there are 43 seats on the coach, how many are spare?

11

10 What colour is a 5 pence coin?

Silver

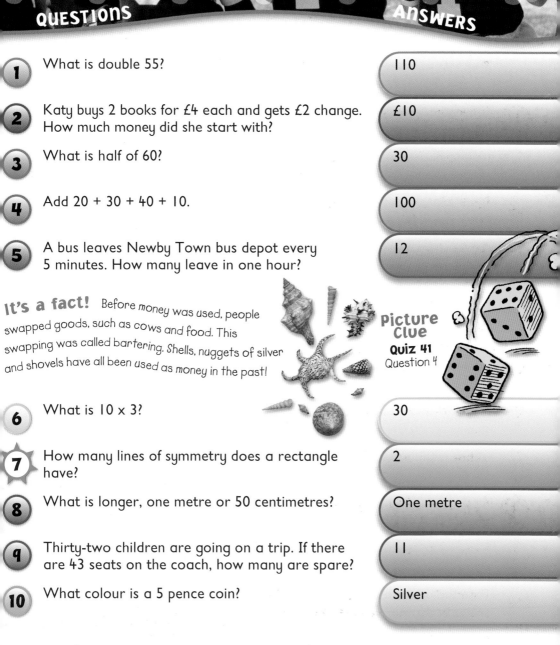

QUESTIONS

ANSWERS

1 How many millimetres are in 2 centimetres?

20

2 I divide 100 pens into 20 pots, putting an equal number in each. How many pens are in each pot?

5

3 Which 3D shape has a circular base and a point at the top?

A cone

4 Charlie's sunflower grows 10 centimetres a week. How tall is the plant when it is 7 weeks old?

70 centimetres

5 What is 2 x 9?

18

It's a fact! A piece of paper can be folded in half, then in half again – but only about ten times. If you had a giant piece of paper that could be folded 50 times it would be bigger than the planet!

Picture Clue
Quiz 44
Question 6

6 What is one-half of a half called?

One-quarter

7 What is the name of an angle that measures 90 degrees?

A right angle

8 Archie had 80 marbles, but lost half of them. How many did he have left?

40

9 Double 25 then divide your answer by five.

10

10 Pete the penguin has twice as many fish as Paula, who has 15 fish. How many fish does Pete have?

30

QUESTIONS

ANSWERS

 1 What word beginning with P is a shape with many straight sides – a polygon or a perimeter?

Polygon

2 Joe has a dentist appointment at 11 a.m. but he is five minutes early. What time does he arrive?

10.55 a.m., or five to eleven

3 How many days are in a normal year?

365

4 How many years are in a decade?

10

 5 Adam had 52 playing cards before he lost 5 of them. How many were left?

47

It's a fact! To find out if a number can be divided by 3, just add up its digits to see if they are a multiple in the 3 times table. For example, 35 can't be divided by three because 3 + 5 = 8, but 27 can because 2 + 7 = 9 (which is 3 x 3).

Picture Clue
Quiz 43
Question 3

6 What word beginning with P is a shape that has 5 corners and 5 sides?

Pentagon

7 What is 5 x 8?

40

 8 How many sides does a 50 pence coin have?

7

 9 How many millilitres are in one litre?

1000 (one thousand)

 10 What number comes next in this sequence: 15, 13, 11 …?

9

Quiz 45 • Number Crunchers

QUESTIONS

ANSWERS

 1 How many shoes are there in 8 pairs?

16

 2 A tortoise travels 3 metres an hour, but a hare travels at 3 kilometres an hour. Which is faster?

The hare

 3 What is one-fourth of a circle?

A quarter

 4 All ants have six legs. How many legs do 10 ants have?

60

5 What is the next number: 95, 85, 75, ...?

65

It's a fact! No two snowflakes are ever the same, but they all form from hexagon-shaped ice crystals.

Picture Clue
Quiz 46
Question 7

 6 Add the number of sides a triangle has to the number of sides a hexagon has.

9

 7 How many minutes are in one hour?

60

 8 Molly's skipping rope is 1.2 metres long, but Amy's is 130 centimetres long. Whose rope is longer?

Amy's

9 What is 10 x 4?

40

10 How many days are in 3 weeks?

21

Quiz 46 • number Crunchers

1 Jamie had £1 but he spent 20 pence on some sweets. How much money did he have left?

> 80 pence

2 What is 25 more than 75?

> 100

3 How many grams are in one kilogram?

> 1000

4 What is 7 x 2?

> 14

5 Which number is biggest: 678, 786 or 768?

> 786

It's a fact! One million has six zeros but one billion has nine zeros. If you write down 1 followed by one hundred zeros you will have written down one googol. Phew!

10000000000000000
0000000000000000
0000000000000000
0000000000000000
0000000000000000
0000000000000000
0000000000

Picture Clue

Quiz 45
Question 7

6 It takes Dad 2 minutes to blow up one balloon. How many could he blow up in half an hour?

> 15

7 How many right angles are there in a square?

> 4

8 How is the volume of petrol measured, in litres or kilograms?

> In litres

9 What is 25 – 15?

> 10

10 How many £2 coins should go into a money bag that is marked £20?

> 10

1 A mother whale weighs 100 kilograms. Her baby weighs half as much. How heavy is the baby?

50 kilograms

2 What is 9 x 5?

45

3 How many corners does a circle have?

0

4 How many minutes are in a quarter of an hour?

15

5 There are 6 eggs in a box. How many eggs are in 2 boxes?

12

It's a fact! A dozen means 12 of something; half a dozen means six. A baker's dozen, however, is 13. Bakers used to sell 13 buns or loaves for the price of 12 to make sure they could never be accused of cheating their customers.

Picture Clue
Quiz 48
Question 1

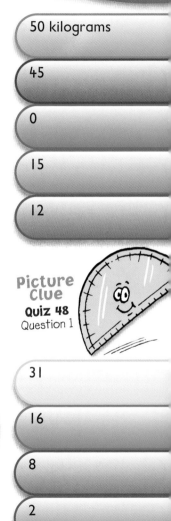

6 What is 41 – 10?

31

7 What is half of 32?

16

8 How many sides does an octagon have?

8

9 Leo makes 8 rolls. Half are ham, one-quarter are cheese and the rest are jam. How many are jam?

2

10 What number comes next in this sequence: 62, 64, 66 …?

68

Quiz 48 • number Crunchers

1 What is half of a circle called? — A semi-circle

2 How many hours are in one day? — 24

3 There are 30 dominoes on the table. Each player takes 10. How people are playing dominoes? — 3

4 There are 100 years in a century. How many years are in 4 centuries? — 400

5 Multiply 3 by 10. — 30

It's a fact! In ancient Rome, people used letters to represent numbers: I = 1, V = 5, X = 10, L = 50, C = 100 D = 500 and M = 1000. From these letters, the Romans could write any number. For example, 58 would have been written LVIII!

Picture Clue
Quiz 47
Question 3

6 A Roman soldier marched 6 kilometres in 2 hours. How long did it take him to march 3 kilometres? — One hour

7 Which is largest: one-quarter or one-third? — One-third

8 Which 3D shape has no edge? — A sphere

9 What is one-quarter of 20? — 5

10 A single bus journey costs £1 and a return ticket costs £1.80. Is it cheaper to get two single tickets, or one return ticket? — One return ticket

Quiz 49 · Number Crunchers

Missing Numbers

Take a look at these number sequences.
Can you work out what the
missing numbers are?

1	10	20	30	40	?
2	9	12	?	18	21
3	41	?	45	47	49
4	99	98	97	?	95
5	100	?	300	400	500
6	?	8	12	16	20
7	25	30	?	40	45
8	2	4	6	8	?
9	21	31	?	51	61
10	75	70	65	60	?

What's the Time, Mr Wolf?

Mr Wolf is still learning how to tell the time. Look at each clock and say whether he is RIGHT or WRONG.

1  Mr Wolf is saying 'Five minutes to six'

6  Mr Wolf is saying '12 o'clock exactly'

2  Mr Wolf is saying 'Eight o'clock'

7  Mr Wolf is saying 'A quarter past six'

3 Mr Wolf is saying 'Twenty to five'

8 Mr Wolf is saying 'Half past eleven'

4 Mr Wolf is saying 'Ten minutes to twelve'

9 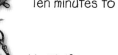 Mr Wolf is saying 'Five to twelve'

5 Mr Wolf is saying 'Five minutes to nine'

10 Mr Wolf is saying 'A quarter to two'

ANSWERS 1. Right 2. Right 3. Wrong (it's twenty to four) 4. Right 5. Wrong (it's 8 o'clock) 6. Right 7. Right 8. Right 9. Wrong (it's five o'clock) 10. Wrong (it's ten to two)

Quiz 51 • Our World

1 What word beginning with C is a large area of land that often includes many countries?

Continent

2 Which Spanish-speaking country borders the United States and is famous for its delicious food?

Mexico

3 What would you buy from a greengrocer?

Fruit and vegetables

4 What is a semi-detached house?

A house attached to one other house

5 Which of these places is the odd one out: Europe, Asia, Japan?

Japan – because it's the only country

It's a fact! People who forecast the weather are called meteorologists (say: meet-ee-or-olo-jists). They study pictures taken by satellites in space to track big storms, such as hurricanes.

Picture Clue
Quiz 52
Question 8

6 I am a place where water comes out of the ground. My water is often clear and clean – what am I?

A spring

7 What does a weather forecaster use to measure temperature – a thermometer or a barometer?

A thermometer

8 What is moving air that travels over land – wind or waves?

Wind

9 Who is the President of the United States?

Barack Obama

10 Which of these two animals is suited to life in a desert – a camel or a crocodile?

A camel

QUESTIONS

ANSWERS

1 What is the name of the burning star in the middle of our Solar System?

The Sun

2 There are over one billion people in my country, and I speak Mandarin. Where do I live?

China

3 How long ago was Britain last covered in a layer of thick ice – 12,000 or 1000 years ago?

12,000 years ago – during the Ice Age

4 Which of these is a type of storm: a hurly-burly, a hurricane or a hutch?

A hurricane

5 What 3D shape best describes the Earth, a sphere or a cone?

A sphere

It's a fact! In AD 79, Mount Vesuvius in Italy erupted. This mighty volcano sent layers of burning ash and poisonous gases over the nearby towns of Pompeii and Herculaneum, killing thousands of people.

Picture Clue
Quiz 51
Question 3

6 What is a wind turbine used for?

To turn wind power into electricity

7 Which layer of gases helps protect Earth from the Sun's burning rays – the no-go zone or the ozone?

The ozone

8 Does it get hotter or colder as you climb up a mountain?

It gets colder

9 Can some types of rock dissolve in rainwater?

Yes, limestone dissolves in water

10 I am a type of mountain and ash, lava and rocks may pour out of my crater. What am I?

A volcano

Quiz 53 • Our World

1 Is an atmosphere a collection of gases or water droplets?

A collection of gases

2 What is a terraced house?

A house attached to others on either side

3 Are quartz, diamond and ruby all types of mineral or metal?

They are all types of mineral

4 What is the capital of France?

Paris

5 Which is bigger, a stream or a river?

A river

It's a fact! Peru borders the Pacific Ocean. Two ancient civilizations – the Norte Chico and the Incas – developed there long ago. The Incas built an amazing city called Machu Picchu.

Picture Clue
Quiz 54
Question 6

6 Who might help you choose a holiday – a travel agent or a traffic warden?

A travel agent

7 Can the heat around a volcano be used to generate electricity?

Yes – this is called geothermal energy

8 What type of shop would you visit to buy medicines or collect them on a prescription?

A pharmacy

9 Where is Peru – South America or Asia?

South America

10 How old are the Caledonian Mountains in Scotland, four million or 400 million years old?

400 million years old

Quiz 54 • Our World

1 What word beginning with V is low land between two mountains?

Valley

2 On which icy, volcanic island did a volcano erupt in 2010, bringing lots of flights to a standstill?

Iceland

3 What is a bungalow?

A house with just one storey

4 What is the area called where the sea meets the land – crest or coast?

Coast

5 Which of these is not a waterfall: Niagara, Victoria or Sahara?

Sahara – it is a desert

It's a fact! Earthquakes are measured on a scale of 1 to 10, with 1 being the least dangerous. A scale of 10 has never been recorded!

Picture Clue
QUIZ 53
Question 2

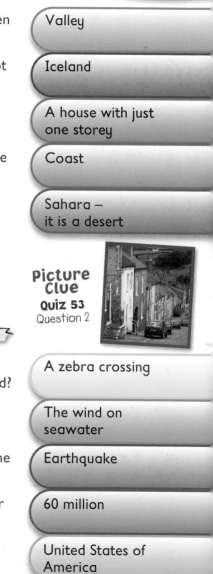

6 What is the name for the black-and-white road markings that show you where to cross the road?

A zebra crossing

7 Are waves caused by the wind on seawater, or the movement of the Moon?

The wind on seawater

8 What name is given to a violent movement of the Earth's crust – volcano or earthquake?

Earthquake

9 What is the population of the UK – 60 million or six million?

60 million

10 What do the letters USA stand for?

United States of America

Quiz 55 • Our World

1 Which planet is sometimes called the Red Planet – Mars or Jupiter?
Mars

2 I live in a country on the other side of the world where there are kangaroos – where do I live?
Australia

3 What is the name of the tallest waterfall in the world?
The Angel Falls (it is 979 metres tall)

4 What do the letters UK stand for?
United Kingdom

5 What is an area of land that is surrounded by water on all sides called?
An island

It's a fact! Canals were built in Britain about 200 years ago to transport goods and connect mines, towns and ports. Canals are still used today, mainly by people enjoying the waterways.

Picture Clue
Quiz 56
Question 7

6 What name is given to rain that has turned into small lumps of ice as it falls?
Hail

7 What is made up of billions of tiny grains of rock particles that often collect on a beach?
Sand

8 What does the Italian word *grazie* mean – thank you or please?
Thank you

9 I am a waterway that is used for moving goods in longboats or barges. What am I?
A canal

10 Is a prairie a type of grassland or lake?
A type of grassland

Quiz 56 • Our World

1 What is a book of maps called?

An atlas

2 What does the French word *merci* mean?

Thank you

3 On what continent would you find the Rocky Mountains – Australia or North America?

North America

4 What is the capital of Ireland?

Dublin

5 What name is given to a slow-moving mass of ice that forms on mountains or near the poles?

Glacier

It's a fact! Deserts are very dry places where less than 25 centimetres of rain falls every year. Antarctica is a vast, frozen landscape that is also a desert.

Picture Clue
Quiz 55
Question 3

6 Is coal a rock that formed from long-dead plants, or a rock that forms inside volcanoes?

A rock formed from long-dead plants

7 What type of animals do farmers keep on dairy farms, cattle or pigs?

Cattle

8 I am in France and I want to buy some bread. Should I look for a *boulangerie* or a *tabac*?

A *boulangerie*

9 What is the largest ocean in the world?

The Pacific Ocean

10 Can deserts be cold?

Yes

Quiz 57 • Our World

1   Name the four seasons there are in one year.

> Spring, summer, autumn, winter

2   Can plastic be recycled?

> Yes, most of it can

3   Is the Arctic Circle at the North Pole or the South Pole?

> The North Pole

4   Which of these would help you find your way if you were lost: a ball of string or a map?

> A map

5   What do the letters GB stand for?

> Great Britain

It's a fact! The Shetland and Orkney Isles are Britain's most northerly places. Meadows and grassy places here are home to wildflowers that can cope with the cold, wet and windy conditions.

Picture Clue
Quiz 58
Question 2

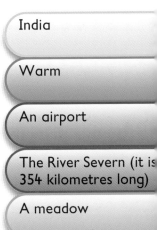

6   I live in Delhi, speak Hindi and follow the Hindu religion. What country do I live in?

> India

7   Are tropical countries mostly warm or cold places?

> Warm

8   Where would you find a runway – at an airport or a sports track?

> An airport

9   What is the name of the UK's longest river?

> The River Severn (it is 354 kilometres long)

10   What is a small area of grassland that often has lots of wildflowers – a meadow or a medley?

> A meadow

Quiz 58 • Our World

QUESTIONS | **ANSWERS**

1 Are the Alps a mountain range in Asia or Europe?

Europe

2 What piece of equipment would you use to look at the planets?

A telescope

3 What is a detached house?

A house that is not attached to any other

4 Is most of the Earth's water salty seawater, or freshwater?

Salty seawater

5 Which enormous rainforest is in Brazil?

The Amazon Rainforest

It's a fact! Orang-utans live in Borneo and Sumatra, in Southeast Asia. Their forest homes are being cut down to make space for farmland, making them very vulnerable to extinction (dying out completely).

Picture Clue
Quiz 57
Question 8

6 What is Ben Nevis – Britain's tallest mountain or its smallest town?

Britain's tallest mountain

7 What type of large shop sells food, clothes and household goods?

A supermarket

8 Is global warming making the Earth a hotter or cooler place?

A hotter place

9 What is the imaginary line that circles the Earth, passing through Africa, Asia and South America?

The Equator

10 Do orang-utans live in forests or grasslands?

Forests

Locate the Landmarks

Can you name these famous landmarks and say in which country they are found?

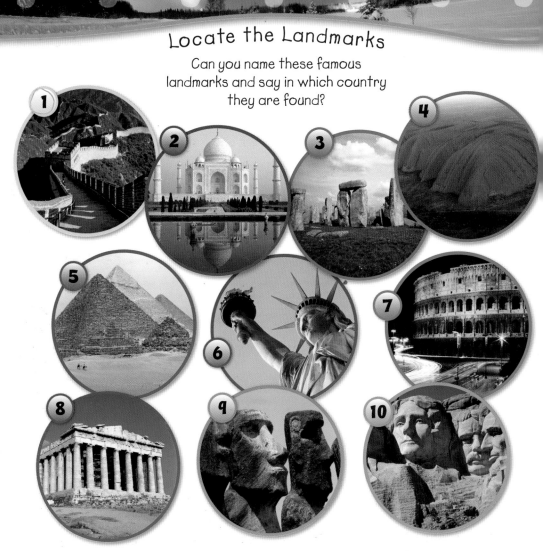

Name the National Dish

Different countries specialize in making different foods, or dishes. See if you can match the food to the country:

China, France, Greece, India, Italy, Japan, Mexico, Spain, United Kingdom, United States.

1 urger

2 Tacos

3 Pizza

4 Sushi

5 Chow mein

6 Quiche

7 Fish and chips

8 Chicken tikka

9 Moussaka

10 Paella

ANSWERS 1. United States 2. Mexico 3. Italy 4. Japan 5. China 6. France 7. United Kingdom 8. India 9. Greece 10. Spain

1 Which ancient people lived in Britain 2000 years ago – the Celts or the Colts?

The Celts

 2 Which famous English king had six wives?

Henry the Eighth

 3 What was the most important fuel in Victorian times – oil or coal?

Coal

 4 Were Nero, Julius Caesar and Hadrian all emperors of Rome or pharaohs of Egypt?

Emperors of Rome

5 Who ruled Britain after the Romans, the Right-Angles or the Anglo-Saxons?

The Anglo-Saxons

It's a fact! Henry the Eighth married six times in total, and had two of his wives executed (their heads were chopped off). He divorced three wives and one luckily outlived him!

Picture Clue
QUIZ 62
Question 10

 6 During the Second World War, what did air-raid shelters help to protect against?

Bombs

 7 Henry VIII destroyed the monasteries. Were they religious places or hospitals?

Religious places

 8 Who was the first man to walk on the Moon, Nigel Armstrong or Neil Armstrong?

Neil Armstrong

 9 Which invaders came from Scandinavia?

The Vikings

10 When was slavery abolished (stopped) in Britain – 1833 or 1933?

1833

Quiz 62 • Past Times

1 When did the Second World War begin – 1993 or 1939?

> 1939

2 Is parchment an old type of clothing or paper?

> Paper

3 On what date is Remembrance Day held every year in the UK?

> 11th November

4 Which ancient people built pyramids and wrapped their dead up as mummies?

> Ancient Egyptians

5 What does a historian study?

> The past

It's a fact! Thomas Edison was a great American inventor who was known as the Wizard of Menlo Park. He invented light bulbs and many other things. His discoveries also led to the invention of movies.

Picture Clue
QUIZ 61
Question 9

6 Was Queen Victoria's husband called King Albert or Prince Albert?

> Prince Albert

7 Who did the Romans worship as the leader of all their gods?

> Jupiter (the Greeks called him Zeus)

8 Mary Seacole was a famous nurse in the Crimean War. Where was she born – Jamaica or London?

> Jamaica

9 What name was given to a ruler of ancient Egypt?

> Pharaoh

10 Where were electric light bulbs invented – the United States or Germany?

> The United States

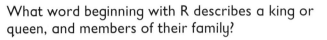

Quiz 63 • Past Times

1 What word beginning with R describes a king or queen, and members of their family?

Royal

2 Which country did Cleopatra rule?

Egypt

3 Why were children evacuated from cities to the countryside in the Second World War?

To keep them safe from bombs

4 What was the name of King Henry Eighth's first wife?

Catherine of Aragon

5 What were Vikings also known as – Norsemen or Celts?

Norsemen

It's a fact! The beginning of human history goes back millions of years. Early humans evolved in Africa, from animals that are also related to chimps and gorillas. Humans eventually spread from Africa around the rest of the world.

Picture Clue
Quiz 64
Question 7

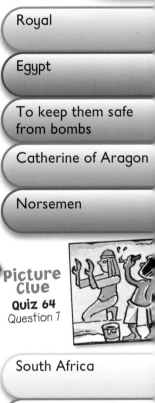

6 In which country was Nelson Mandela born?

South Africa

7 Was Elizabeth Fry famous for her work in helping people in prison, or for nursing soldiers?

Helping people in prison

8 What do British people celebrate on the fifth of November?

Bonfire night

9 Does a coronation take place when a king or queen is crowned or buried?

Crowned

10 Which Roman invaded Britain – Julius Caesar or Marcus Brutus?

Julius Caesar

Quiz 64 • Past Times

QUESTIONS

ANSWERS

1 Were the Romans from Europe or America?

Europe (Rome is in Italy)

2 What is the name of the Queen's home in London?

Buckingham Palace

3 Was Alfred the Great an Anglo-Saxon ruler or a Tudor king?

Anglo-Saxon ruler

4 Who has not been the Prime Minister: Gordon Brown, Tony Blair or Jenson Button?

Jenson Button

5 Which sporting games began in Greece nearly 3000 years ago?

The Olympic Games

It's a fact! Between AD 700 and 1100, Vikings left their homelands in Scandinavia and went exploring in their longboats. They travelled to find new lands and treasure.

Picture Clue
Quiz 63
Question 8

6 In which country was the first skyscraper built?

The United States

7 Which ancient people wrote using hieroglyphics?

Ancient Egyptians

8 In what century was the first aeroplane invented, the 18th century or the 20th century?

20th century

9 Who did the Vikings attack when they came to Britain, the Romans or Anglo-Saxons?

The Anglo-Saxons

10 What was William Shakespeare famous for?

Writing plays and poetry

Quiz 65 • Past Times

 1 What type of boat did the Vikings use?

Longboat

 2 Is a locomotive a type of train or plane?

Train

 3 When sirens sounded during the Second World War, why did people go to air-raid shelters?

To stay safe while bombs dropped

 4 When was Elizabeth II crowned Queen – 1983 or 1953?

1953

 5 Who was Christopher Columbus?

A famous explorer

It's a fact! The Rosetta Stone revealed the meaning of hieroglyphs (ancient Egyptian writing). You can see it, and other historical artefacts from around the world, at the British Museum.

Picture Clue
Quiz 66
Question 2

6 Was Henry the Eighth a Tudor or Stuart king?

A Tudor king

 7 Where can people go to see treasures and historical documents?

A museum

 8 What hopping game did Victorian children like to play?

Hopscotch

 9 Where was the 'Wild West' – the United States or Russia?

The United States

 10 Which deadly disease carried by fleas on rats killed millions of people in the Middle Ages?

The plague (the Black Death)

Quiz 66 • Past Times

QUESTIONS

ANSWERS

1 Did Britain fight in the First World War?

Yes

2 Which ancient people built villas that were decorated with mosaics?

The Romans

3 When was the Battle of Hastings – 1066 or 1966?

1066

4 What started in Pudding Lane, London in 1666?

The Great Fire of London

5 Did Victorian children work in coal mines?

Yes, they did

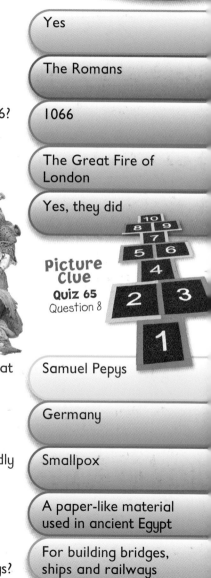

It's a fact! When Europeans first explored America it was already inhabited. The Europeans called the people they met 'Indians', because they thought they had landed in India!

Picture Clue

Quiz 65 Question 8

6 Which famous diary-writer wrote about the Great Fire of London – Anne Frank or Samuel Pepys?

Samuel Pepys

7 Which country did Adolf Hitler rule during the Second World War?

Germany

8 Edward Jenner was an English doctor. What deadly disease did he treat, smallpox or chicken pox?

Smallpox

9 What was papyrus?

A paper-like material used in ancient Egypt

10 Is Isambard Kingdom Brunel famous for painting horses or building bridges, steamships and railways?

For building bridges, ships and railways

Quiz 67 • Past Times

 1 Which ancient people held gladiator fights?

The Romans

 2 Which British sailor explored the Pacific in the 18th century – Captain Cook or Captain Hook?

Captain Cook

 3 What do Americans celebrate on July 4th every year – Yogi Bear Day or Independence Day?

Independence Day

 4 How did King Henry the Eighth's second wife, Anne Boleyn, die?

Her head was chopped off

5 Who was the English king during the Crusades – Richard the Lionheart or Boris the Brave?

Richard the Lionheart

It's a fact! In Greek myths, the Minotaur was a monster with the body of a man and the head of a bull. It was kept in an underground maze and was eventually killed by a man called Theseus.

Picture Clue
Quiz 68
Question 6

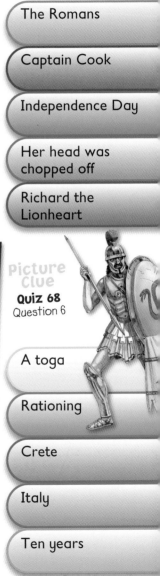

6 What was a Roman robe called – a yoga or a toga?

A toga

7 What word beginning with R describes the way food was shared out during the Second World War?

Rationing

 8 Where did the ancient Minoans live – Crete or Mexico?

Crete

9 Christopher Columbus was a famous explorer. Was he born in Italy or India?

Italy

 10 How long did the Trojan War last – two days or ten years?

Ten years

Quiz 68 • Past Times

1 Which English queen fought the Spanish Armada?

Elizabeth the First

2 What did British farmers rely on to plough fields before machines were used – horses or sheep?

Horses

3 Roughly how many years did the Romans rule in Britain – 400 or 40?

400

4 What did early trains use as fuel – coal or gas?

Coal

5 Who invented fireworks – the French or the Chinese?

The Chinese

It's a fact! During the Trojan War, the Greeks built a big wooden horse. They hid inside the horse, which the Trojans wheeled into their city. Once inside, the Greeks jumped out and destroyed Troy.

Picture Clue
Quiz 67
Question 6

6 Was Achilles a Greek warrior or Roman soldier?

A Greek warrior

7 Did the Anglo-Saxons use bricks and mortar or wattle and daub to build their homes?

Wattle and daub

8 Who fought the British at the Battle of Waterloo – Louis the Sixteenth or Napoleon Bonaparte?

Napoleon Bonaparte

9 The Rocket was invented by George Stephenson. Was it a steam locomotive or a space ship?

A steam locomotive

10 Who won the battle of Hastings in 1066 – William the Conqueror or Henry the Eighth?

William the Conqueror

Old and New

Group these objects in sets of two,
so you have one old and one new.

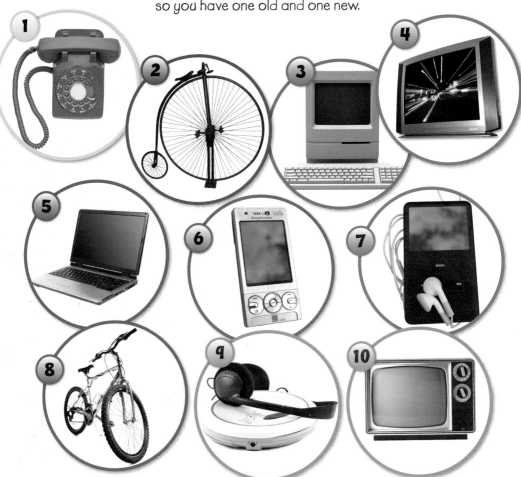

Quiz 70 · Past Times

Historical Fighters

See if you can match the pictures of the
warriors to their names below:

American Indian, Aztec, Celt, Commando, Gladiator,
Greek hoplite, Knight, Samurai, Viking, Zulu.

1 I work in people's houses, fixing boilers and water systems. What is my job?

Plumber

2 What travel document do you need to take with you when you go abroad?

Passport

3 In what season are harvest festivals – autumn or spring?

Autumn

 4 Which game was invented by the Aztec civilization of Mexico – ice hockey or field hockey?

Field hockey

 5 I am 77 years old and I no longer work. Am I attired or retired?

Retired

It's a fact! There are more than 400 castles in Wales. Most were built to protect people from attackers.

Picture Clue
Quiz 72
Question 4

 6 What word beginning with H is a pastime or sport, such as collecting stamps or sailing?

Hobby

 7 What do the letters UN stand for – Unfair Notions or United Nations?

United Nations

8 How many languages are spoken in Africa – 100 or 1000?

1000

9 What is Dame Ellen MacArthur famous for – sailing or swimming?

Sailing

 10 What word beginning with C is a big, stone building with a moat and drawbridge?

Castle

QUESTIONS

ANSWERS

 1 Who should be the first medical person to arrive at an accident – a paratrooper or a paramedic?

A paramedic

 2 Which of these is not a games console: Wii, Xbox 360, Jax 2020, PS2?

Jax 2020

3 What building is a Christian place of worship?

A church

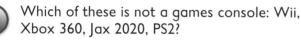 **4** If a German person wishes you 'Guten Appetit!' what are they saying?

Enjoy your meal ('Good appetite')

5 What word beginning with L describes rubbish thrown on the ground rather than put in a bin?

Litter

It's a fact! The native people of New Zealand are called Maoris. Europeans settled there about 200 years ago and it was ruled by Britain for a while.

Picture Clue
Quiz 71
Question 3

 6 Jewish people have a festival called Sukkot – is it a time of celebration or sorrow?

Celebration

7 When people live in the country are they described as living a rural life or a ragged life?

A rural life

 8 What was the name of Prince William's and Prince Harry's mother – Diana or Margaret?

Diana

9 What do we call the group of people who run the whole country – the council or the government?

The government

10 Are New Zealand's farmers well known for keeping sheep or ostriches?

Sheep

QUESTIONS

ANSWERS

 1 I make patients comfortable, help doctors and give out medicine. What is my job?

A nurse

 2 Who celebrates the festival of Easter – Christians or Jews?

Christians

 3 Which Australian people play the didgeridoo – Incas or Aborigines?

Aborigines

 4 Where is St Paul's Cathedral – Leeds or London?

London

 5 What word beginning with S is a type of wrestling that is very popular in Japan?

Sumo

It's a fact! St Paul's Cathedral was designed by Sir Christopher Wren. It was built where an earlier church had burnt down in the Great Fire of London in 1666.

Picture Clue
Quiz 74
Question 5

 6 Where would you go to enjoy the work of Pablo Picasso – an art gallery or the theatre?

An art gallery

 7 On what continent do Brazilians live – South America or Africa?

South America

 8 Who founded the Scout movement – Lord Baden-Powell or the Duke of Wellington?

Lord Baden-Powell

 9 Which disease kills more people around the world than any other – heart disease or gum disease?

Heart disease

 10 What word beginning with J is a city in Israel that is holy to Jews, Christians and Muslims?

Jerusalem

1 What parts of the body does a manicurist look after?

Hands and nails

 2 What is the name for a Muslim place of worship?

Mosque

 3 What is Leona Lewis famous for?

Singing

4 What is the area where you, and the people around you, live – a common or a community?

Community

5 What is the UK's national anthem called?

God Save the Queen

It's a fact! Leona Lewis is a successful British singer who was born in 1985. She became famous after winning a talent show on TV.

Picture Clue
Quiz 73
Question 3

 6 I wear loose white robes and a coloured belt. What sport do I play – judo or ludo?

Judo

7 In which city are the Houses of Parliament?

London

8 What pop group did Alesha Dixon perform with?

Mis-Teeq

 9 Which famous Time Lord did David Tennant play in a BBC television series?

Doctor Who

 10 In which country would you expect to hear people speaking Mandarin – Denmark or China?

China

1. I make sure a football game is played fairly and safely. What is my job?

Referee

2. I attend a synagogue and I celebrate Hannukah – am I a Sikh or a Jew?

A Jew

3. Whose job is it to stop crimes being committed and to catch people who break the law?

The police

4. What material does a carpenter work with – wood or metal?

Wood

5. Does the UK have a President or a Prime Minister?

A Prime Minister

It's a fact! The first police officers were known as 'peelers' or 'bobbies' after Sir Robert Peel, who set up London's Metropolitan Police Force in 1829.

Picture Clue
Quiz 76
Question 6

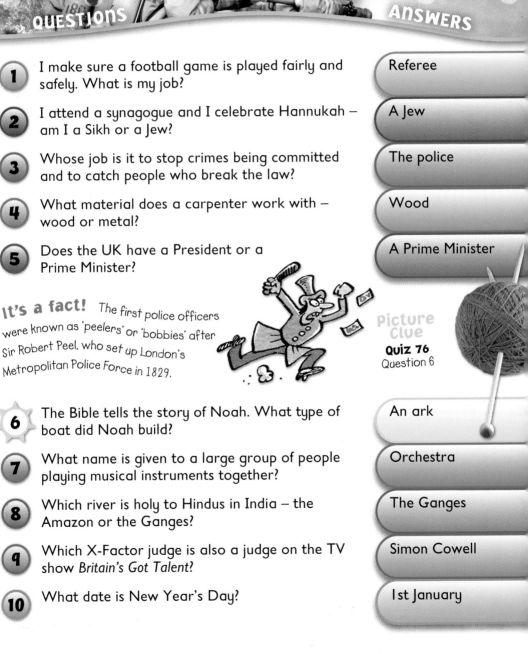

6. The Bible tells the story of Noah. What type of boat did Noah build?

An ark

7. What name is given to a large group of people playing musical instruments together?

Orchestra

8. Which river is holy to Hindus in India – the Amazon or the Ganges?

The Ganges

9. Which X-Factor judge is also a judge on the TV show Britain's Got Talent?

Simon Cowell

10. What date is New Year's Day?

1st January

Quiz 76 • How We Live

 1 What is the Jewish holy day called?

Shabbat (or Sabbath)

 2 Which charity helps animals and protects them from cruelty – the RSPCA or the RNLI?

RSPCA

 3 Is Adele a British or American singer?

British

 4 What is the most common religion in India – Hinduism or Christianity?

Hinduism

 5 How many singers are in the boy band JLS?

Four

It's a fact! The Royal Society for the Prevention of Cruelty to Animals (RSPCA) is a charity that was set up in 1824. It tries to ensure that animals live healthy, safe lives.

Picture Clue
Quiz 75
Question 6

 6 For what handicraft does a person use two large needles and a ball of wool?

Knitting

 7 Where is a chef most likely to work – in a bookshop or a restaurant?

In a restaurant

 8 How many birthdays does the Queen have?

Two: A real one and an official one

9 Are Ganesh and Krishna gods of the Hindu or Buddhist faiths?

Hindu

10 I work at night, mixing tunes. I keep up with the latest music. What is my job?

A DJ (Disc Jockey)

Quiz 77 • How We Live

 1 What liquid do women spray to make themselves smell nice?

Perfume

 2 What is the name of the Muslim holy book?

The Qu'ran

 3 What word beginning with V is something people do at an election?

Vote

 4 What date is Christmas Eve?

24th December

 5 If a French person wishes you 'Bon appétit!' what are they saying?

Enjoy your meal ('good appetite')

It's a fact! The Union Jack is the flag of the United Kingdom of Great Britain and Northern Ireland. It combines the flags of Scotland, England and Ireland.

Picture Clue
Quiz 78
Question 2

 6 Which of these people are not Europeans – Belgians, Scots or Australians?

Australians

 7 What does an angler catch?

Fish

 8 Where are people sent to when they commit crimes?

Prison

 9 What is the British flag known as – the Union Jack or Union Jill?

Union Jack

10 Which type of money do Americans use – dollars or Euros?

Dollars

1 I check that cars are parked correctly and that parking charges are paid. What is my job?

Traffic warden

2 What is the top medal someone can win at the Olympic Games – bronze, silver or gold?

Gold

3 What name is given to a place where people are buried – a celebrity or a cemetery?

A cemetery

4 What word beginning with V is a person who deliberately damages other people's property?

Vandal

5 What day of the week is most holy to Christians?

Sunday

It's a fact! France is a very popular place to visit and makes more money from tourism than any other country apart from the United States and Spain.

Picture Clue

Quiz 77
Question 6

6 Is an engagement the time before two people get married, or just after they get married?

Before they get married

7 Which is the most visited country in the whole world – Canada or France?

France

8 Who do postmen and women work for – the Royal Mail or the National Post?

The Royal Mail

9 What is the author J K Rowling famous for writing?

The Harry Potter books

10 My family celebrates Diwali. Am I a Hindu or a Christian?

A Hindu

Parlez-vous Français?

Do you know what these French words
mean? If not, the pictures might help you!

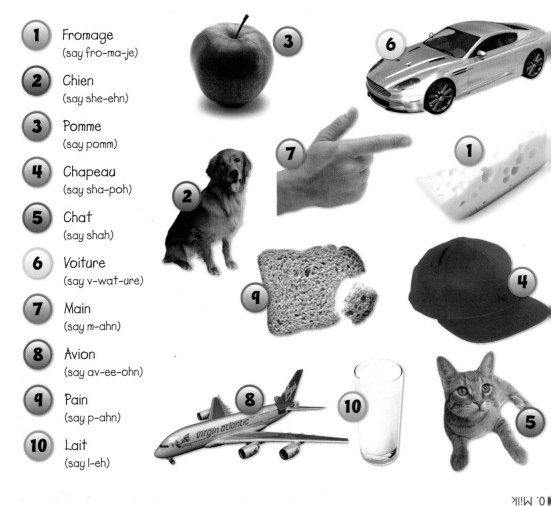

1. Fromage
(say fro-ma-je)

2. Chien
(say she-ehn)

3. Pomme
(say pomm)

4. Chapeau
(say sha-poh)

5. Chat
(say shah)

6. Voiture
(say v-wat-ure)

7. Main
(say m-ahn)

8. Avion
(say av-ee-ohn)

9. Pain
(say p-ahn)

10. Lait
(say l-eh)

ANSWERS 1. Cheese 2. Dog 3. Apple 4. Hat 5. Cat 6. Car 7. Hand 8. Aeroplane 9. Bread 10. Milk

Where in the World?

Look at the list below. Can you match the
continents and oceans to the numbers on the map?

Africa, Antarctica, Asia, Atlantic Ocean, Europe,
Indian Ocean, North America, Oceania,
Pacific Ocean, South America.

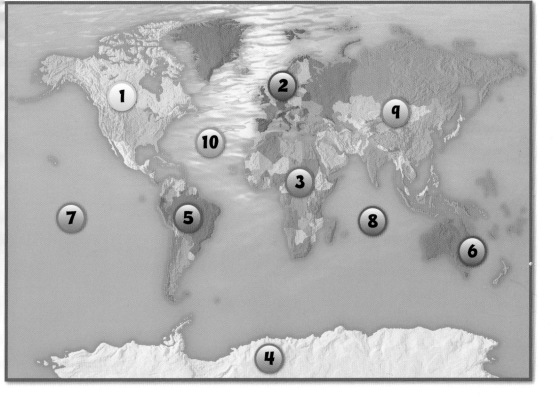

ANSWERS 1. North America 2. Europe 3. Africa 4. Antarctica 5. South America 6. Oceania 7. Pacific Ocean 8. Indian Ocean 9. Asia 10. Atlantic Ocean

 1 Julius Caesar had a pet giraffe.

True

 2 Rice grows in flooded fields, known as paddy fields.

True

 3 Children only have one kidney, but adults have two.

False. Everyone has two kidneys

 4 In 1830, a child as young as five could work underground in coal mines.

True

 5 Copper, silver and gold are all types of metal found in rocks.

True

It's a fact! In Victorian times, children had to work to bring money into the family. They worked on farms, in shops, as servants and down coal mines. They were paid 25p a week, or less.

Picture Clue
Quiz 82
Question 2

 6 Four babies are born around the world every single second.

True

 7 Tiny micro organisms, such as bacteria, help dead things to rot.

True

 8 'Bonjour' is the Spanish word for 'hello'.

False. It is the French word for 'hello'

 9 Turquoise is a shade of orange.

False. It is a shade of blue/green

 10 Rubber balls bounce better than bean bags.

True

1 It takes 50 times more energy to make a battery than the finished battery contains.

True

 2 Most plants can move – they turn towards sunlight.

True

 3 The Summer Olympics take place every year.

False. They happen every four years

4 More than one million earthquakes happen every year.

True, but most are very small

5 Roman soldiers were sometimes paid in salt.

True

It's a fact! Stonehenge is an enormous circle built from large stones. Ancient Britons created it as a holy place about 5000 years ago.

Picture Clue
Quiz 81
Question 6

 6 About half the people who live in Africa are under the age of 15.

True

 7 Bicycle tyres are hard because they have concrete inside them.

False. They have air inside them

8 Stonehenge is older than the Egyptian pyramids.

True

 9 If you sneeze with your eyes open your eyeballs will pop out.

False

 10 All electricity in the country is turned off for one hour at night to save energy.

False

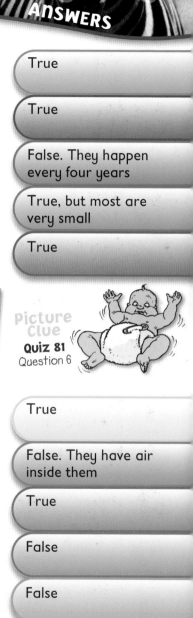

Quiz 83 • True or False

QUESTIONS

ANSWERS

1 The Earth is like a giant magnet.

True. That's why a compass points north

2 Cats and dogs are colour blind.

False. They can see some colours

3 Violins can have 6, 8 or even 12 strings.

False. Violins have just four strings

4 Flour, eggs, milk and cheese are used to make Yorkshire puddings.

False. Cheese is not in Yorkshire puddings

5 Waterfalls can be used to make electricity for homes.

True

It's a fact! Hydroelectricity is made using flowing water. It is a much cleaner way of making electricity than using fossil fuels, such as coal, oil and gas.

Picture Clue
Quiz 84
Question 3

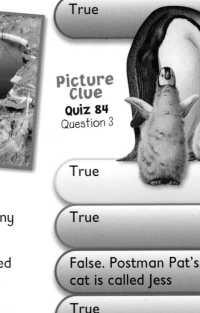

6 The people of ancient Crete jumped over bulls for fun.

True

7 People in Britain eat more chocolate than any other nation.

True

8 Postman Pat has a black-and-white cat called Mog.

False. Postman Pat's cat is called Jess

q Add 27 to 28 and you get a total of 55.

True

10 Flexible things are bendy.

True

Quiz 84 • True or False

1 Some snakes can swallow African elephants whole.

False. Elephants are much too big

2 Madrid is the capital of Spain.

True

3 Emperor penguins can fly from one end of the Antarctic to the other.

False. Penguins can't fly

4 Stinging nettles can be used to make soup.

True

5 Yeast is used to make cheese.

False. It is used to make bread

It's a fact! About 13 billion plastic bottles are thrown away in the UK every year. Most plastic bottles can be recycled.

Picture Clue
Quiz 83
Question 2

6 The umbrella was invented in Scotland.

False. It was invented in China

7 Mirrors can reflect images because they have a layer of shiny metal inside them.

True

8 Throwing plastic bottles and bags away is a good idea because they make homes for small wildlife.

False. Litter is dangerous to wildlife

9 It can get so hot around volcanoes that mud bubbles and water boils.

True

10 More than half of the people in the world live in cities.

True

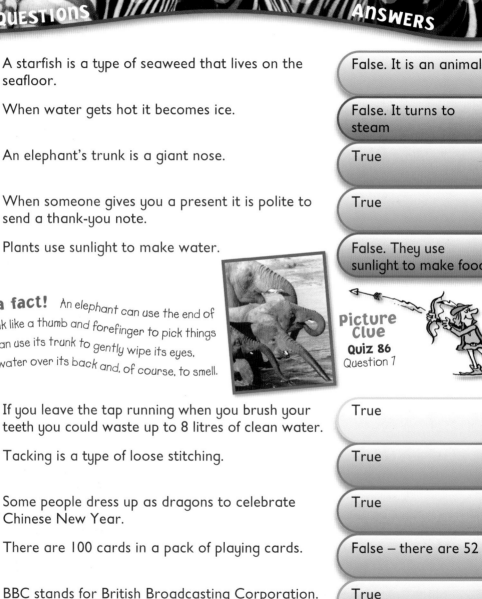

Quiz 85 • True or False

1 A starfish is a type of seaweed that lives on the seafloor.

False. It is an animal

2 When water gets hot it becomes ice.

False. It turns to steam

3 An elephant's trunk is a giant nose.

True

4 When someone gives you a present it is polite to send a thank-you note.

True

5 Plants use sunlight to make water.

False. They use sunlight to make food

It's a fact! An elephant can use the end of its trunk like a thumb and forefinger to pick things up. It can use its trunk to gently wipe its eyes, spray water over its back and, of course, to smell.

Picture Clue
Quiz 86
Question 7

6 If you leave the tap running when you brush your teeth you could waste up to 8 litres of clean water.

True

7 Tacking is a type of loose stitching.

True

8 Some people dress up as dragons to celebrate Chinese New Year.

True

9 There are 100 cards in a pack of playing cards.

False – there are 52

10 BBC stands for British Broadcasting Corporation.

True

Quiz 86 • True or False

1 Pasta grows on trees.

False – it is made from wheat

2 You can find red giants and white dwarves in space.

True – they are types of star

3 Animals that are hunted by others are called prey.

True

4 Scientists have found water on planet Mars.

True

5 Slugs may look stupid but scientists have taught them how to spell.

False

It's a fact! Mars is the most similar planet to our own. Scientists have found frozen water on its surface – meaning life may once have existed there.

Picture Clue
Quiz 85
Question 8

6 An outfit worn by an actor or actress on stage is called a dressing-gown.

False. It is called a costume

7 Robin Hood stole from the poor to give to the rich.

False. He stole from the rich to give to the poor

8 Your family name is also called your surname.

True

9 Africa is a country.

False – it is a continent

10 If you mix black and white paints together you get blue.

False – you get grey

Quiz 87 • True or False

 1 Before paper was invented people wrote on dried animal skin.

True – it was called vellum

 2 A river flows from its mouth to its source.

False. It flows from the source to the mouth

 3 Sheep are herbivores, which means they only eat plants.

True

 4 The world's biggest Hindu shrine is called Angkor Wat.

True

 5 According to legend, St George killed the Minotaur.

False – he killed a dragon

It's a fact! Angkor Wat in Cambodia is an ancient Hindu place of worship built around 1000 years ago. Historians believe a city grew up around the temple.

Picture Clue
Quiz 88
Question 1

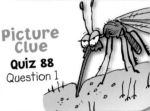

 6 When something freezes, it goes from being a solid to a liquid.

False – it turns from a liquid to a solid

 7 Someone who uses a bow and arrow is called an archer.

True

 8 A square has eight lines of symmetry.

False – it has four

 9 Athletes have to swim, cycle and run when they take part in a marathon.

False – it is just a running race

 10 A good raincoat should be absorbent.

False – it should be waterproof

Quiz 88 • True or False

1 One of the world's deadliest diseases is carried by a flying insect.

True. Mosquitoes spread Malaria

2 Elephant poo can be used to make paper.

True

3 The Apollo 11 mission took people to the Moon for the first time in 1972.

False – it was 1969

4 Pitch, beat and volume are all words that are used to describe music.

True

5 Half of 74 is 38.

False: It is 37

It's a fact! In 1969, the Apollo 11 mission landed on the Moon, and two astronauts walked on its surface. In 1972, the Apollo 17 mission returned, but no one has walked on the Moon since.

Picture Clue
QUIZ 87
Question 3

6 Giant worms live deep in the oceans.

True

7 A spatula is a tool used for cooking.

True

8 Bats are birds with fur rather than feathers.

False – they are mammals, not birds

9 The world's largest desert is the Sahara in Africa.

True

10 Shetland, Welsh and Dartmoor are all types of pony.

True

Quiz 89 · True or False

Animal Names

Look at the pictures and names of the animals below. Answer true if you think the names are correct and false if you think they are wrong.

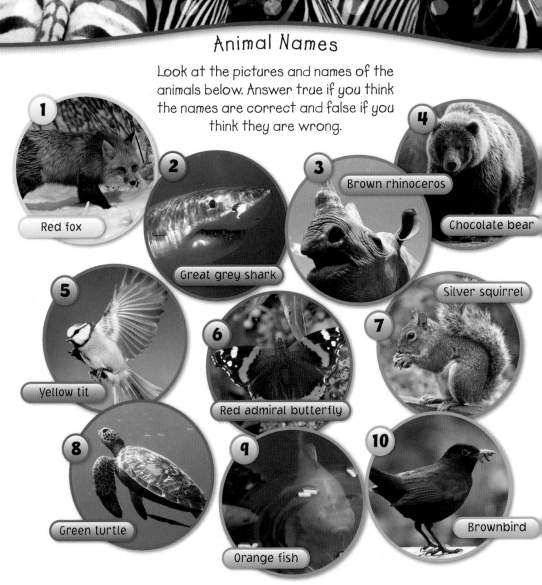

1. Red fox
2. Great grey shark
3. Brown rhinoceros
4. Chocolate bear
5. Yellow tit
6. Red admiral butterfly
7. Silver squirrel
8. Green turtle
9. Orange fish
10. Brownbird

Quiz 90 • True or False

Animal Armies

A collective noun is a word used to describe a group of something, for example a herd of sheep. Are these collective nouns real, or made up? Look at each one and answer true or false.

1. A mob of meerkats

2. A colony of walruses

3. A lounge of lions

4. A school of dolphins

5. A gallop of horses

6. A brood of chickens

7. A troop of chimpanzees

8. A gaggle of geese

9. A congregation of crocodiles

10. A buzz of bees

ANSWERS 1. True 2. False – a herd or a pod of walruses 3. False – a pride of lions 4. True 5. False – a herd of horses 6. True 7. True 8. True 9. True 10. False – a swarm of bees

Quiz 91 • Lucky Dip

QUESTIONS

ANSWERS

 1 What word beginning with P is an orange vegetable often used as a Halloween decoration?

Pumpkin

 2 Are elephants bigger or smaller than blue whales?

Smaller

 3 What is another word for pieces of information – nuggets or data?

Data

 4 What is the longest key on a computer keyboard called – the space bar or the thumb key?

The space bar

5 How many musical notes are in an octave?

Eight

It's a fact! Halloween is a traditional festival that is celebrated on 31st October. People like to dress up, have parties and decorate their homes with pumpkins.

Picture Clue
Quiz 92
Question 8

 6 Which mythical horse has a horn on its head?

Unicorn

7 Which TV presenter has appeared on *Top Gear* and *Brainiac* and has his own *Blast Lab* on CBBC?

Richard Hammond

 8 What is connected to a computer and loaded with paper and ink?

Printer

 9 How many semi-circles make one circle?

Two

  10 In which UK country could you visit Dundee, Aberdeen, Perth and Glasgow?

Scotland

Quiz 92 • Lucky Dip

QUESTIONS

ANSWERS

1 Which swimming stroke is the fastest – front crawl or backstroke?

Front crawl

2 What word beginning with D means to remove text on a computer screen?

Delete

3 What colour is a ruby?

Red

4 What would you do to a tambourine – play it or eat it?

Play it

5 Where would you find catkins – in woodlands or at a vet's surgery?

In woodlands. They grow on trees

It's a fact! Rubies are precious stones that have formed in the Earth's crust. They can be cut and polished to sparkle and gleam and then used in jewellery.

Picture Clue
Quiz 91
Question 10

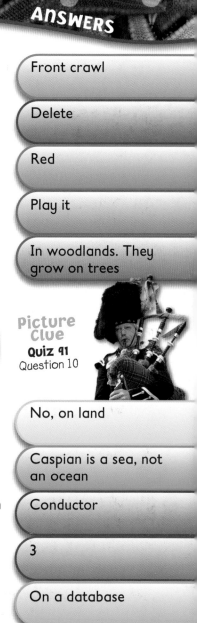

6 Do crocodiles lay their eggs in water?

No, on land

7 Which of these is not an ocean: Arctic, Indian, Caspian or Atlantic?

Caspian is a sea, not an ocean

8 Who holds a baton, reads music and organizes an orchestra?

Conductor

9 6, 9 and 12 are all multiples of what number?

3

10 In a computer, where would you find files, records and fields – on a database or in a picture file?

On a database

Quiz 93 • Lucky Dip

QUESTIONS

ANSWERS

1 What is the name of a long loaf of French bread — a baguette or a bagel?

A baguette

2 What type of graphic might you use to show data – a lemon tart or a pie chart?

A pie chart

3 In which UK country could you visit Bangor, Swansea and Cardiff?

Wales

4 Was Archimedes a Greek maths genius or an Italian sculptor?

A Greek maths genius

5 What is the bony framework that supports our bodies called?

The skeleton

It's a fact! Actress Emma Watson plays Hermione Granger in the Harry Potter movies. Despite being busy with filming, Emma kept up her school work and went to university.

Picture clue
Quiz 94
Question 2

6 What number is five less than 872?

867

7 Where would you find a SIM card?

In a mobile phone

8 Is Hermione Granger a witch or a muggle in the Harry Potter stories?

A witch

9 What name is given to artwork made from bits of paper or other materials stuck on a background?

Collage

10 What does the 'e' stand for in 'email'?

Electronic

Quiz 94 • Lucky Dip

QUESTIONS

1 What is the missing suit: clubs, diamonds, hearts and…?

2 In which movies would you find a squirrel called Scrat living in a cold climate?

3 How many balls are on a snooker table at the beginning of a game – 22 or 42?

4 What do the letters PC stand for – private console or personal computer?

5 Is graffiti scribbling on a wall, or an Italian pasta dish?

It's a fact! There are 52 cards in a pack of modern playing cards. The cards are divided into four suits of 13 cards each.

6 If there are six zeros in one million, how many zeros are in one trillion?

7 Which battle did Admiral Lord Nelson fight – the Battle of Trafalgar or the Battle of the Bulge?

8 What type of music did Handel write – classical or hip-hop?

9 If you have a bird's eye view of something can you see it from above or from the front?

10 Which key do you press on a keyboard to start a new line?

ANSWERS

Spades

The *Ice Age* movies

22

Personal computer

Scribbling on a wall

Picture Clue
Quiz 93
Question 8

12

The Battle of Trafalgar

Classical

From above

The return or enter key

QUESTIONS

ANSWERS

1 What do the letters www in an Internet address stand for?

World wide web

2 Where will the 2016 Olympics be held?

Rio de Janeiro, Brazil

3 If you cut a shape into six equal parts, what is each part called?

One-sixth

4 Which medicines can kill bacteria – antifreeze or antibiotics?

Antibiotics

5 Who wrote *Alice in Wonderland* – Lewis Carroll or Michael Morpurgo?

Lewis Carroll

It's a fact! Marco Polo was born around 1254 and lived in Venice, Italy. He was one of the first Europeans to travel to China and Mongolia.

Picture clue

Quiz 96
Question 6

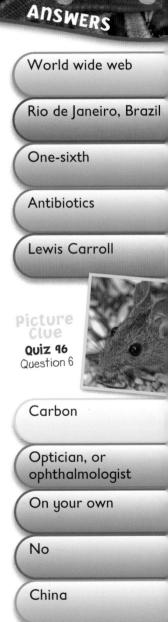

6 Which of these is not a gas – oxygen or carbon?

Carbon

7 Which word beginning with O is a person who checks your eyesight?

Optician, or ophthalmologist

8 If you do something 'solo' are you part of a team or on your own?

On your own

9 Do jellyfish have bones?

No

10 Marco Polo was an explorer. Did he travel to China or to Canada?

China

Quiz 96 • Lucky Dip

QUESTIONS

ANSWERS

 1 Which word beginning with S is the art of making figures or objects from material such as stone?

Sculpture

 2 Would you blow into an oboe, or strum its strings?

Blow into it

3 Which letter sits between A and D on a computer keyboard – S or P?

S

 4 When is twilight – at the middle of the day or at the end?

At the end

5 Round up the number 47 to the nearest ten.

50

It's a fact! One of the most famous sculptures can be found in Paris. It is called The Thinker and was made by Auguste Rodin. It was finished in 1902 and presented to the public in 1904.

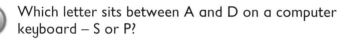

Picture Clue
Quiz 45
Question 9

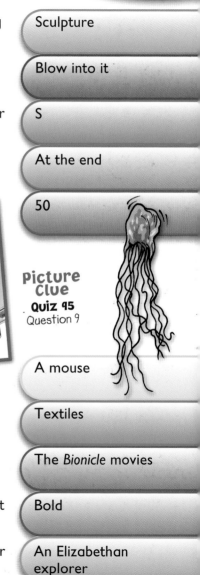

 6 Which computer gadget would you 'right click'?

A mouse

 7 Which word beginning with T describes fabrics that you might use in art – textiles or taxes?

Textiles

8 Which movies feature the mighty character of Mata Nui?

The *Bionicle* movies

 9 Which word beginning with B means to make text darker or more obvious on screen and in print?

Bold

 10 Was Sir Francis Drake an Elizabethan explorer or a priest?

An Elizabethan explorer

QUESTIONS

ANSWERS

 1 What word beginning with N is a thin piece of metal that you use to sew?

Needle

 2 What word is used to describe a group of ants – a mob or a colony?

A colony

 3 In legend, on which mountains can the Yeti be found – the Pennines or the Himalayas?

The Himalayas

 4 What is the world's biggest continent – Europe or Asia?

Asia

 5 Is oregano a fruit or a herb?

A herb

It's a fact! There are many creatures that people believe in, even though no one has proved they exist. Creatures such as fairies and mermaids, and monsters like the Yeti, appear in folk tales across the world.

Picture Clue

Quiz 98
Question 10

 6 Spell 'magical'.

Magical

 7 When was the microwave oven invented – the 1840s or the 1940s?

The 1940s

 8 In which popular cartoon series does Yugi appear?

Yu-Gi-Oh!

 9 If a Spanish person says 'Que aproveche!' are they telling you to enjoy your meal, or go to bed?

Enjoy your meal

 10 Is 9752 an even number or an odd number?

An even number

Quiz 98 • Lucky Dip

 1 What is the Jewish holy book called?

The Torah

 2 Where would you put a memory stick – into a computer or under your pillow?

Into a computer

3 In which UK country could you visit Manchester, Cambridge and Leeds?

England

 4 Which word beginning with P is a number that can only be divided by one or itself?

Prime number

 5 Which cartoon characters love Wensleydale cheese and had adventures with a were-rabbit?

Wallace and Gromit

It's a fact! Jules Léotard was a French acrobat and trapeze artist. The leotard, which was named after him, is a stretchy one-piece outfit that allows people to move freely.

Picture Clue
Quiz 97
Question 2

 6 What colour do you get when you mix red and yellow paints together?

Orange

 7 How does an animal get energy – by hibernating or by eating?

By eating

 8 What would you use to measure speed – kilograms an hour or kilometres an hour?

Kilometres an hour

 9 Which superhero is known as Peter Parker in his everyday life?

Spiderman

10 Who might wear a leotard – a gymnast or a clown?

A gymnast

Making Music

See if you can name the musical instruments from the list below?

Banjo, clarinet, electric guitar, harmonica, harp, saxophone, sitar, steel drum, trombone, trumpet.

ANSWERS 1. Saxophone 2. Trumpet 3. Trombone 4. Clarinet 5. Harmonica 6. Steel drum 7. Harp 8. Sitar 9. Banjo 10. Electric guitar

Quiz 100 • Lucky Dip

Out and About

Can you name all these different
forms of transport?

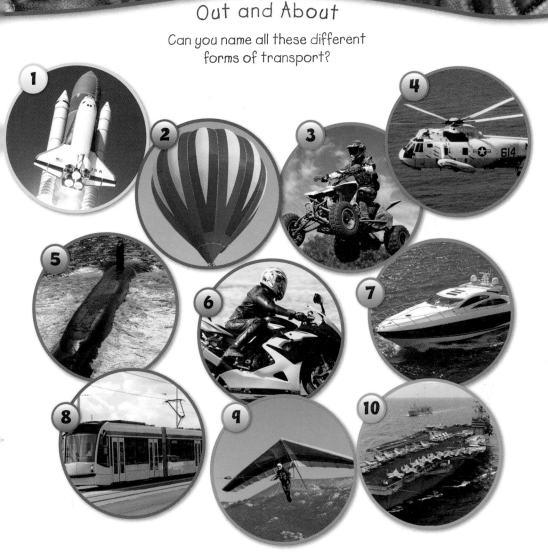

SCORECARDS

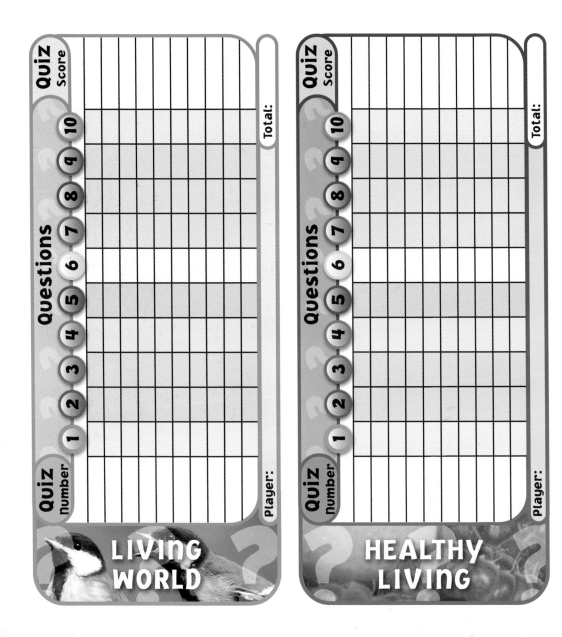

LIVING WORLD

Quiz number	Questions										Quiz Score
	1	2	3	4	5	6	7	8	9	10	

Player: Total:

HEALTHY LIVING

Quiz number	Questions										Quiz Score
	1	2	3	4	5	6	7	8	9	10	

Player: Total:

Photocopy the scorecards instead of writing in the book, so you can play again and again. Don't forget – for each section, you'll need one scorecard for each player. See pages 6–7 for help on how to play.

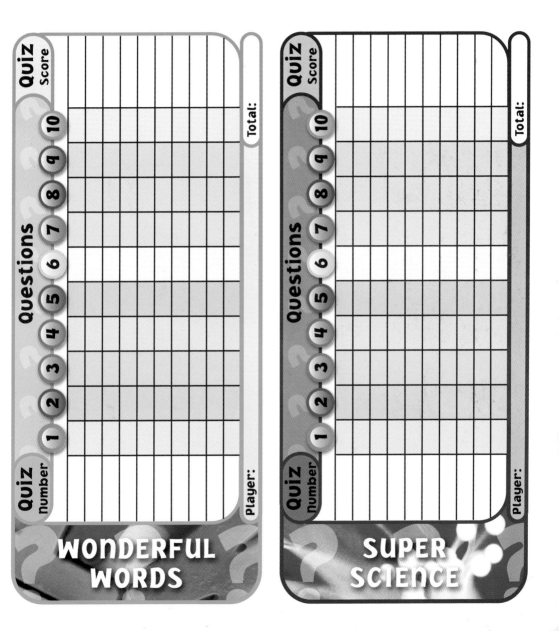

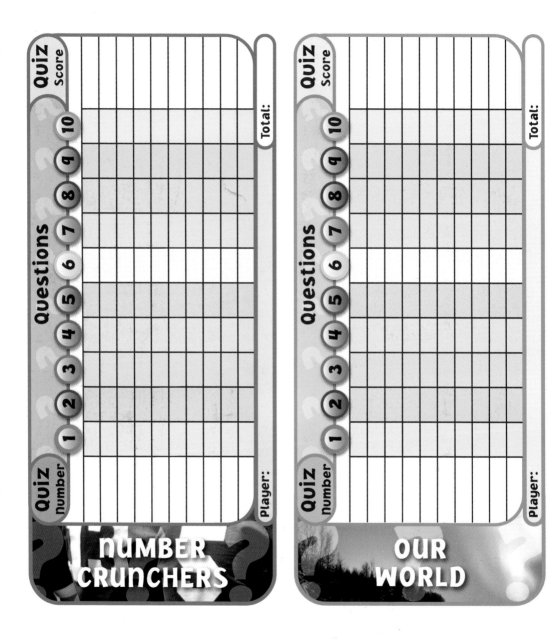

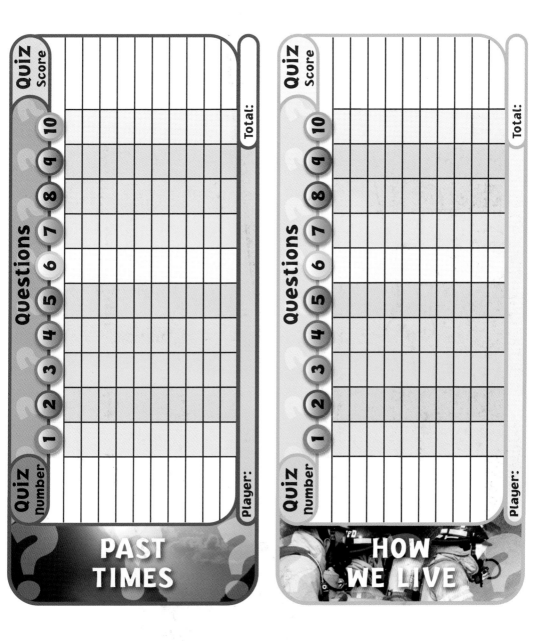

PAST TIMES

Quiz number | Questions | Quiz Score
1 2 3 4 5 6 7 8 9 10

Player: | Total:

HOW WE LIVE

Quiz number | Questions | Quiz Score
1 2 3 4 5 6 7 8 9 10

Player: | Total:

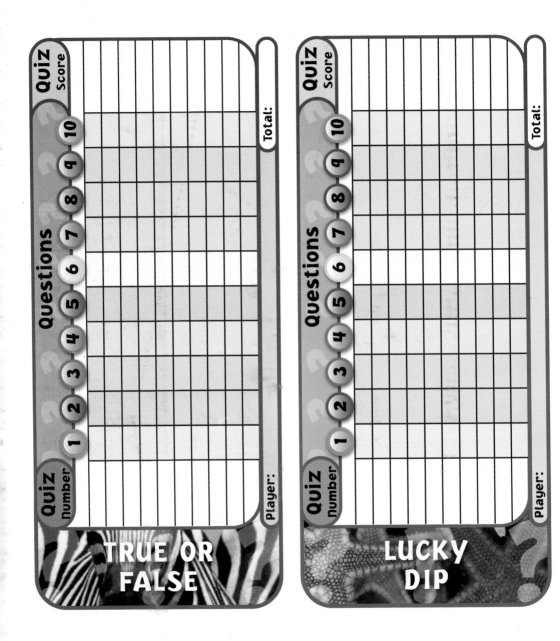